Change
and Your Relationships:
A Mess Worth Making

STUDY GUIDE
WITH LEADER'S NOTES

Timothy S. Lane and Paul David Tripp

New
Growth
Press
WWW.NEWGROWTHPRESS.COM

Change and Your Relationships: A Mess Worth Making

New Growth Press, Greensboro, NC 27404
Copyright © 2009 by Timothy S. Lane and Paul David Tripp
All rights reserved. Published 2009.

Cover Design: The DesignWorks Group, Nate Salciccioli and Jeff Miller, www.designworksgroup.com
Typesetting: Lisa Parnell, lparnell.com

ISBNs: 978-1-942572-53-4

Printed in the United States of America

26 25 24 23 22 21 20 19   5 6 7 8 9

Contents

Acknowledgments

We (Paul Tripp and Tim Lane) would like to express our gratitude for those who have made this resource a reality. The content for this resource began with the book *Relationships: A Mess Worth Making*. The editing skill of Sue Lutz was vital for the completion of that book.

Change and Your Relationships was crafted by the editing skills of Michael Breece. Thank you, Michael, for your solid work and your contribution to this new resource. We hope many people will be helped as they work through these lessons and apply them to their lives and relationships.

We would also like to thank New Growth Press for their investment in this resource. Thanks to Mark and Karen Teears for your ongoing efforts to take CCEF material and create resources that will equip the body of Christ to grow in grace. We are thankful for our partnership in the gospel. Thanks to Barbara Juliani for her persistent administrative oversight to see this project to completion.

Finally, thanks to all the individuals and churches who have shared their stories of how the book *Relationships: A Mess Worth Making* has helped them grow in wisdom in their personal relationships. We hope that this user-friendly resource will help many more as they walk through these lessons. May they find the grace of Christ richly and practically applied to their own lives as they study this material with others.

A Word of Welcome

Welcome to *Change and Your Relationships*. We are thankful for your desire to grow in this very crucial area of your life. When you think about it, we all spend a majority of our waking hours interacting with people. These interactions, both casual and more personal, have the potential to shape us—either for good or ill. Relationships are always a two-way street!

As you work through *Change and Your Relationships*, it is our hope that you will learn to think more clearly about the primary purpose of relationships and how important they are in conforming us to the likeness of Christ. This key idea of being conformed to Christ can and should radically reorient the way we think about our friendships, marriages, relationships with our children and parents, our neighbors, coworkers, and everyone in between.

Perhaps a few words would be helpful about this course you are about to take:

1. This resource is connected to several other CCEF resources, including *How People Change* and *Instruments in the Redeemer's Hands* (both of these are books and small-group resources such as this one). *Change and Your Relationships* places the important process of change within its primary context: our relationships! While this may seem obvious, one danger that exists when we talk about personal change is turning inward and forgetting that personal change occurs in the bigger context of our relationships, so all personal change must also affect the way we treat others. This emphasis on living out gospel change in our relationships makes this resource a helpful complement to the other resources from CCEF that focus on personal change.

2. This resource is intended to point you toward a radically biblical understanding of relationships. For many, including these authors, relationships can easily become conduits for personal satisfaction and self-centered happiness. While God does want us to find great joy in our friendships, he never states that as the end goal or primary motivation. Rather, he places his purpose for us at the center: becoming more like Christ. The more God's agenda for relationships lives at the center of our motivation for pursuing relationships, the more likely it is that we will have good relationships, but it does not necessarily guarantee that all of our friendships will be fulfilling. Instead of looking to your relationships to fulfill you, it is our hope that this curriculum will enable you to see the bigger picture of what God is accomplishing in and through your relationships—one that is much grander than your personal happiness. This resource might disappoint those who are looking for several easy steps to more effective and happy friendships, but it will be a great encouragement to those who learn to set their sights on the sanctifying work of the Father, Son, and Spirit.

3. Our greatest hope is that this resource will provide a way for individuals, marriages, and entire churches to be transformed into communities that are growing in bringing together seemingly contradictory things like candor and compassion, humility and courage, patience and godly conflict. "Godly conflict" may sound like a strange thing to hope for—that is, unless you have seen too much ungodly conflict! It is only through God's Spirit powerfully working in the lives of many individuals that these kinds of communities can emerge. The authors of this material claim no special ability, personally, when it comes to these things—certainly not because we write about it! But we do stand with all who will study this material and say with confidence that progress and movement can and will be made as we embed our lives more deeply in the gospel of grace that is ours in Christ. Our Trinitarian God is one God and three persons. There is unity and diversity. He is a social God, and we are a relational people. It is by his design that this *is* true, and it is only by his grace that it *will be* true of us.

Thank you for your interest in the ministry of CCEF and for using this resource that we trust will help you and many others. It is our privilege to partner with you and to have a small or significant role in your growth in grace. After all, "So neither he who plants nor he who waters is anything, but only God, who makes things grow. The man who plants and the man who waters have one purpose, and each will be rewarded according to his own labor. For we are God's fellow workers; you are God's field, God's building" (1 Cor. 3:7–9).

Timothy S. Lane and Paul David Tripp

Relationships and the Nature of God

Central Point and Application

Central Point: Because God himself is a community, he created and intends for us to live in community so that we may be a reflection of him.

Personal Application: I need to be properly involved in relationships.

Relational Application: I need to be in close relationship to God because my relationships with others will be satisfying only if I am in relationship with God.

THE BIG QUESTION
Do you see and treat relationships as God intends for you?

Opening Activity

For five minutes, brainstorm any words that come to mind when you hear the word *relationships*.

Relationships can be messy. Having to deal with flawed people in a broken world can make one wonder if some relationships are even worth it. Have you felt this way? Have you ever avoided a neighbor or a co-worker? Ever choose to just swallow how you really feel because the work involved, if you really opened up, doesn't seem worth it?

The difficulty of relationships can lead to families sharing the same space without sharing meaningful contact, church meetings becoming a formality with no attempt to share in the lives of others, and neighbors living side by side without knowing anything significant about one another. Is this a valid way to live? Is it OK to keep to ourselves so that we don't get hurt or don't hurt someone else? What's wrong with playing it safe?

Oddly enough, we can live with a tension between self-protective isolation and the desire for meaningful relationships. We can, on one hand, avoid the discomfort often created by relationships but, at the same time, know that we are less than human when we are alone. Every relational decision we make tends to move toward either isolation or immersion, and sometimes we may find ourselves at an extreme end of this continuum; we are tempted to make relationships either less or more than they were intended to be.

"I want to be safe" ◄———► "I need you in order to live"
(isolation)   (immersion)

1. Which side of the continuum do you tend to move toward? Why?

Relational Profiles

Because we tend toward one of these characteristics—immersion or isolation—our relationships tend to fit one of three profiles:

1. The Frustrated Relationship: In this relationship, one person moves toward isolation and the other moves toward immersion. One dreams of being safe; the other dreams of being close and intimate.

   a. How would the perfect vacation look to each of these two types of people?

   b. How might it feel to live in this type of relationship?

2. The Enmeshed Relationship: Here both people move toward immersion. Both parties are relationally dependent on the other.

   a. How would the perfect vacation look to each of these two types of people?

b. How might it feel to live in this type of relationship?

3. The Isolated Relationship: In this relationship both persons move toward isolation. Both make relational decisions based on maintaining safety.

    a. How would the perfect vacation look to each of these two types of people?

    b. How might it feel to live in this type of relationship?

When things go wrong in relationships, the problem is often rooted in the heart and in the expectations we bring to the relationships, whether it is our expectation for safety or for dependency. This is why we need to seek *God's* expectations for our relationships: What purpose does God intend relationships to serve in our lives? As persons created in the image of God, what should our relationships look like? Without a biblical model to explain the place relationships should have in our lives, we will likely experience imbalance, confusion, conflicting desires, and general frustration.

Our Communal God

Since we are made in the image of God, we cannot talk about the nature of human relationships without first thinking about the nature of God.

Read John 17:20–26.

1. For whom and for what is Jesus praying in this part of his prayer?

2. What is the model for community Jesus sees for his people?

3. If God himself is a community, what does it mean to be human, made in God's likeness?

4. In Christ's prayer, what is one of the purposes for human community?

5. Why do we need Christ to be praying for us?

6. Christ not only prays for our unity with one another but that we would also have community with whom?

7. Is there anything else about this prayer and its background that shows God's deep commitment to creating true community?

8. Think about the stages of a person's life beginning from birth. What can you identify that shows we were designed to be in community with others?

Closing Activity

Look at the list of words brainstormed for the opening activity; identify any words that should be the focus of our thoughts about relationships. Are there any words you feel should be added?

1. Are there any relationships in your life, including perhaps your relationship with God, you need to correct your perspective on?

God designed us to be relational—it is our very nature, and it is one way in which we reflect the image of God. And *only* when we live in community do we fully reflect the likeness of God. Relationships are not optional! Because of sin, relationships can be messy, but they are not optional. Problems in relationships are often rooted in our selfish desires—when we seek to fulfill our own perceived wants and needs instead of seeking to please God. If there are problems in your relationships, the solution starts with God; the circle of human community is only healthy when it exists within the larger circle of community with God.

Central Point

1. We are less than human when we are alone.
2. We are tempted to make relationships more or less than they were intended to be.
3. God, the Trinity, is a community; as his creation we reflect this quality, and only when we live in community do we fully reflect the likeness of God.

Personal Application

1. I need to acknowledge that God desires me to be properly involved in relationships.
2. I need to identify whether I tend toward isolation or immersion.

3. I need to admit that good relationships with others flow from good communion with God.

Relational Application

1. I need to be in relationship with others, neither avoiding nor depending upon them.
2. I need to find balance between isolation and immersion.
3. I need to be, first and foremost, in relationship with God.

Make It Real

1. Who are people in your life (family, work, neighborhood, church, etc.) you feel you should be building better relationships with? What will it require for you to build and improve these relationships?

2. What are your expectations for your closest relationships?

3. If there are problems in your relationships, the solutions begin with God. Identify and write down any problems you have in your relationships.

4. Spend time with your spouse, close friends, small group, and so forth, and share your answers to the items below:

Share whether you feel there are any problems in your relationship. (Do not share what you feel the problems are, only whether you feel there are or are not problems.)

Rate the problems (without naming the problems) on a scale of 1 (minor) to 10 (major).

Identify whether you tend toward isolation or immersion.

Identify whether your relationship tends to be (1) frustrated, (2) enmeshed, or (3) isolated.

Identify, using a percentage, how much you relate to the other person(s) in a way intended to please God.

Share with one another what you learned about relationships in this lesson, including (1) how important are relationships to God? (2) from where does true human community grow?

Relationships— The Problem and the Solution

<u>Review</u>

How important are relationships to God? From where does true human community grow?

Did you work on any relationships this past week?

Did you share your answers from Make It Real question 4 in lesson 1?

Central Point and Application

Central Point: Our problems in relationships have everything to do with sin inside us, and our potential to overcome the problems has everything to do with Christ.

Personal Application: I need to look inward to my heart to identify my part of a conflict.

Relational Application: I need to seek restoration in a godly way that includes searching my own heart and confessing my sin to the other person.

THE BIG QUESTION
Where do the problems in relationships lie, and can they be repaired?

Opening Activity

Ask yourself these simple questions:

- Have you ever felt misunderstood?
- Have you ever been hurt by what another person said?
- Have you ever felt as if you haven't been heard?
- Have you ever been betrayed?
- Have you ever had to work through a misunderstanding?
- Have you ever disagreed on a decision?
- Have you or the other person ever held a grudge?
- Have you ever experienced loneliness even when things were going well?
- Have you ever been let down?
- Have you ever doubted another person's love?
- Has the other person ever doubted your commitment?
- Have you ever struggled to resolve a conflict?
- Have you ever wished that you didn't have to give or serve?
- Have you ever felt used?
- Have you ever thought, *If I had only known?*

Even in our most satisfying relationship, we can probably answer yes to all of these questions. Even in our most satisfying relationship, there are struggles and temptations, quarrels and conflicts. If we can answer yes to most of these questions for our *best* relationship, how much more work must be required in relationships that are more difficult! Our experiences with relationships help us understand why the Bible includes so many commands and exhortations to be patient, kind, forgiving, compassionate, gentle, and humble. The Bible assumes that relationships this side of eternity will be messy and require a lot of work.

Inside Out, Upside Down

James asks, "What causes fights and quarrels among you?" and answers by reminding us that our real problem is not located outside ourselves (which we can be so easily tempted to blame) but is rather inside us: "Don't they come from your desires that battle within you?" (James 4:1). We allow our selfish desires to rule over us instead of God, and this leads to problems, conflicts, and disappointments. This role reversal—making ourselves ultimate and God secondary—the Bible calls sin.

Exploring the Problem

Finish each of these lines with a word or phrase:

Sin inside of me is like a _____

_____ .

Sin inside of me makes me feel like a _____

_____ .

When I think of my sin, I feel _____

_____ .

When I think of my sin, I need _____

_____ .

Read Romans 7:21–25.

1. Identify some words or phrases Paul uses to describe his sinful condition.

Conclusion: Our biggest problem is inside us, and we can't repair it on our own.

The Basic Effects of Sin

Kristin and Shane had been friends since grade school. In high school, something more than friendship began to blossom. Although they ended up at different colleges, they remained close and spent at least three weekends a month together.

It wasn't long before they began to talk about marriage. They felt so fortunate to marry someone who had been a friend since childhood! The college years flew by, and soon after graduation, they married. They looked forward to spending the rest of their lives together.

Shane and Kristin found good jobs and purchased a beautiful home in a neighborhood they loved. Their days were busy, but their evenings together were wonderful. They always looked forward to their Saturday brunch at the bohemian café down the street. It seemed as if they were living their dream when, unexpectedly, Kristin was pregnant. This was not part of the plan. She had tried to be careful! What in the world would she tell Shane?

Kristin dreaded seeing Shane and answering the question he was sure to ask. She wanted him to be understanding, maybe even excited, but she knew this was unlikely. That conversation was a turning point in their relationship. Shane was very upset that Kristin "hadn't been more careful." Kristin was crushed that Shane would blame the pregnancy on her and treat the baby like a disease. On top of this, Kristin and Shane desperately needed her income, but if she continued to be sick as she had been, she wouldn't be able to work for long. Shane was discouraged, Kristin was sick, and their finances were growing tighter every day.

Their struggles soon began to erode their relationship. Shane became bitter, frustrated, critical, and demanding. He worked more at the office and seemed to be more occupied at home with office matters too. Kristin pulled away from Shane, giving him space, and spent more time with her girlfriends. Having been raised in a well-managed, financially stable family, Shane was irritated that they had gotten themselves into such a tight spot. Kristin was hurt that her closest friend now seemed like her worst enemy.

Shane and Kristin's biggest problem is inside them—not the unexpected pregnancy and financial difficulty. If Shane and Kristin see the unexpected circumstance as the root of their problem instead of their own sin, then they will continue to struggle in their relationship.

Sin erodes relationships by affecting us in six basic ways. Let's identify these eroding influences in Shane and Kristin and then in ourselves.

1. Self-centeredness: Since relationships are about being other-centered, the self-centeredness of sin will inevitably subvert God's design. When we reject God, we create a void that cannot remain empty. Sin will lead us instinctively to fill it with ourselves.

   a. Can you identify self-centeredness in Kristin and Shane's relationship?

2. Self-rule: When God's wise and loving rule over us is replaced with self-rule, other people become our subjects. They are expected to

do our bidding and bow to our control. Because relationships are supposed to be conducted between two people who are equally submitted to God, the quest for self-rule will always wreak havoc.

a. Can you identify the sin of self-rule in Shane and Kristin's difficulty?

3. Self-sufficiency: When we reject God, we believe the intoxicating but poisonous delusion that we are not dependent. If we don't see that we are dependent upon God, it is unlikely that we will be humbly dependent on others. One of God's principle means of providing for us is through our human relationships.

a. How have Kristin and Shane moved toward self-sufficiency?

4. Self-righteousness: When the holiness of God is not our personal standard of what is good, true, and right, we will always set ourselves up as that standard, leading us to develop an inflated view of ourselves and an overly critical view of others. Godly relationships flourish best between two humble people who acknowledge their weaknesses and sins and their need for grace.

a. Can you identify self-righteousness in Shane and Kristin?

5. Self-satisfaction: When we convince ourselves that satisfaction can be found apart from God, we can move in two different directions. We can try to find satisfaction in material things, which will lead to a disinterest in relationships or using them as a means to get what we want; or we can try to find satisfaction in people, using relationships for our own happiness.

a. How have Shane and Kristin turned to self-satisfaction?

6. Self-taught: When we are our own source of truth and wisdom, we forsake the humble, teachable spirit that is vital to a good relationship. We always take the role of mentor and give the impression that we have little if anything to learn from others.

a. How do you see this attitude in Shane and Kristin?

We said earlier that relationships can be a means of diagnosing our own weaknesses. The following chart summarizes the effects sin has on a person and his or her relationships. Using this chart, make a diagnosis of your own sinful condition.

	Seeks/ Wants	Acceptable Cost	Nightmare/ Fear	Others' Experience	Telltale Emotion/ Action
Self- Centeredness	Attention, approval	Will sacrifice control and independence	Rejection, not being recognized or affirmed	Others feel used, minimized, smothered	Anxious, needy
Self- Rule	To be right, in control	Will sacrifice intimacy and unity	Being seen as wrong, being dependent	Others feel coerced, manipulated	Angry
Self- Sufficiency	Independence, time alone	Will sacrifice intimacy, mutually helpful community	The dependence and neediness of others	Others feel ignored, unappreciated	Cold, distant
Self- Righteousness	Being right in the eyes of others	Will sacrifice relationships that challenge or confront	Being wrong, guilty, or condemned	Others feel challenged, condemned, or dismissed	Aggressive, argumentative
Self- Satisfaction	Pleasure (self-defined)	Will sacrifice community if inconvenient	Others interfering with personal pleasure	Others feel like objects, not companions	Controlling, demanding, dissatisfied
Self- Taught	A platform for one's own opinion	Will sacrifice growing together if you disagree	Being told what to think, say, and do	Others feel patronized, disrespected	Opinionated, domineering

Whenever the things we want (false gods) become more important than God, even when we make relationships more important than God, our relationships suffer. The circle of human relationships was meant only to exist within the larger circle of community with God.

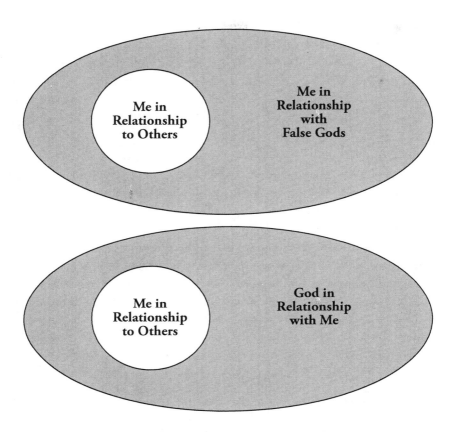

What About the Bad Things People Do to Me?

What we have said so far may give the impression that our relationships are only harmed by *our* sin. But the Bible is full of exhortations calling us to exercise patience, forbearance, compassion, forgiveness and love; to revoke revenge and anger. The Bible mentions these things because God knows we will be sinned against. Like Shane, we are sometimes the victimizers; and like Kristin, we are sometimes the victims; and then there are times when we are both.

Even when we are sinned against, we are still responsible for how we react. We all tend to sin in response to being sinned against, adding trouble to our trouble. Can you identify with any of these responses to being sinned against?

- I confess your sins to myself with bitterness: *I can't believe she did that to me!*
- I confess your sins to another person in gossip: *Let me tell you what she did to me!*
- I confess your sins to God, seeking vengeance: *God, when are you going to do something to the person who hurt me?*
- I confess your sins to you in anger: *How dare you do such a thing to me?*

The Bible reminds us that even when we are sinned against, ultimately, before God, our biggest problem is still our own hearts' propensity to sin. Even when our hearts have been horribly damaged by the sins of others, we are to guard our hearts so that we are not sucked into sin's destructiveness. Being sinned against tempts us to sin. So our need for Christ is as big when we are sinned against as it is when we sin. God does not call us to passivity when we are sinned against, but our response is to be with patience, gentleness, self-control, humility, and forgiveness; not in vengeance, gossip, bitterness, or with a grudge. Holding the perpetrator "accountable" with a sinful spirit ends up perverting the very justice you seek.

Perhaps the messiness of relationships feels overwhelming. Is there any hope for restoration or for godly relationships?

1. What has God given us to help us navigate relationships in a fallen world?

Two Mistakes

If we feel overwhelmed or have lost hope, we may be making two mistakes.

1. We may be thinking God's grace is supposed to deliver us from problems, when, in reality, God's grace often gives us the ability to persevere in the midst of problems. We desire the grace of relief while God gives the grace of empowerment.

2. We may be measuring our potential to deal with difficulty by the size and duration of the problems instead of measuring our potential according to the size of God's provisions. Even in the deepest difficulty, we are never without resources and never apart from God's presence.

Our problems have everything to do with sin, and our potential has everything to do with Christ!

Shane and Kristin did find grace for their struggle. They sought help. Listening to the other talk about his or her hurts was very difficult at first. But as they faced their struggle, they also saw something else. They began to see their God, not off in the distance somewhere but right there with them in the difficulty. As they began to trust him, they began to find the courage to trust each other again and continue to move toward each other.

Closing Activity: Exploring the Solution

Finish each of these lines with a word or phrase:

Christ inside of me is like a _____

_____ .

Christ inside of me makes me feel like a _____

_____ .

When I think of Jesus, I feel _____

_____ .

When I think of Jesus, I need _____

_____ .

Central Point

1. On this side of eternity, relationships will be messy and require a lot of work.
2. Our biggest problem in relationships is inside us.
3. We need God's grace in our relationships.

Personal Application

1. I need to expect difficulties in my relationships.
2. I need to examine my own heart and confess my sins that either lead to the conflict or resulted from the conflict.
3. I need to depend on God's grace to persevere and not my own wisdom or strength.

Relational Application

1. I shouldn't be angry when difficulties come; they are a part of life and God's tool for spiritual growth.
2. I need to seek restoration in a godly way that includes searching my own heart and confessing my sin to the other person.
3. I need to seek restoration knowing God will provide grace to get through it.

Make It Real

1. When you encounter issues in your relationship, do you immediately focus on outside problems or the inside problems of your heart? What could you do as a couple or as a group to help each other focus first on the sin problems of your heart?

2. Share your diagnosis from the chart with someone else. Invite that person to ask you weekly how you are doing identifying that sin and confessing it.

3. Identify a relationship that is most difficult for you. Has your attitude toward the relationship changed since doing this lesson? How has it changed and why? Or why has it not changed?

4. Do you feel hopeful in your difficulties or overwhelmed? What can you do to maintain the hope? What can you do if you are still feeling overwhelmed?

5. Have you made one or both of the "Two Mistakes"? What can you change so that you are no longer in error?

Preparation for Lessons 3 and 4: In Ephesians 4:1 Paul says we are to "live a life worthy of the calling you have received." Read the first three chapters of Ephesians, and make a list of the things we have received from God and a list of things we are called to.

EPHESIANS 1–3
Things We Have Received

EPHESIANS 1–3
Things We Are Called To

Relationships— God's Workshop

Review

What is the problem in any relationship? Where does the solution lie?

Share one of your responses from Make It Real lesson 2.

Central Point and Application

Central Point: God uses relationships to lead us into growth and sanctification.

Personal Application: I need to make God's purpose for relationships my purpose as well.

Relational Application: I need to take relationships seriously as a gift from God and work through the issues in relationships in order to grow and become more like Jesus.

THE BIG QUESTION
In your relationships, whose agenda will you seek, God's or your own?

Opening Activity

The following statements are good and show positive areas in a relationship, but can you identify the underlying agenda in these statements?

- "I am so happy we don't argue like we used to."
- "I just love being with you."
- "It's great to know that I have found someone I can trust."
- "We have such a great sex life."
- "Before I met you, I was so lonely."

A wealthy celebrity has just given a sizable donation to a worthy cause. During an interview he is asked, "What motivated you to make this donation?" At first glance the gift seems to be a generous act of kindness. But the celebrity answers, "When I wake up in the morning, I can look at myself in the mirror and say that I am a good person. And when I go to bed at night, I can feel good about myself." No doubt the donation will benefit others, but the point is that what looks good on the surface doesn't always look that way under closer inspection. What we get out of them can "drive" even our most altruistic moments.

Two Scriptural Themes

Two themes about relationships predominate in Scripture:
1. The power of self-interest is still present in the believer. While the control of sin is broken, the sin that remains in us still puts up a real fight. We will never escape the power of self-interest in this life, even in our best relationships. In fact, the more satisfying the relationship, the less conscious you will be of self-interest. The most destructive diseases are the ones that don't show themselves in obvious ways. This is true of spiritual maladies as well.
2. God has a bigger agenda for our relationships than we do.

   a. What is your dream for your relationships?

In all things God has a purpose and design. God's purpose and design for relationships is to conform us to the image of Christ! Does this match with your dream?

Ephesians 4: God's Desire for Our Relationships

We all have a dream for our relationships; and because our dream is often what we want, in the way we want, and at the time we want, it tends to lead to impatience, vengeance, lying, manipulation, envy, competition, disgust, hostility, or anger. Ephesians 4 shows us what God wants our relationships to be.

Read Ephesians 4:1.

Paul urges us to "live a life worthy of the calling you have received." Our lives should reflect this calling we have received! Specifically, Paul says it should show up in our relationships in the body of Christ. In other words, you can't take the gospel seriously and not take your relationships seriously.

As we consider this passage (Eph. 4), ask yourself whether this is how you think about your relationships. It may be helpful to use this list to think about one particular relationship.

A Call to Unity

Read Ephesians 4:1–6.

"Maintain the unity of the Spirit." Paul says we are to maintain— not create—these relationships. If we are Christians, we automatically are in relationship with other Christians. We are united with other believers because we are united with Christ and share the same Spirit. Therefore, our relationships are gifts to be managed and taken care of. Gossip, slander, anger, and so on, devalues and harms these gifts. If we are willing to pursue, forgive, and serve, we demonstrate care for these gifts. Is there a relationship you struggle to see as a gift? If so, are you willing to ask God to change your heart and perspective?

"Make every effort." What is it about hard work that can be satisfying? Paul knows that relationships, even among people who have the Spirit, will not be easy. The biblical work ethic for relationships is that it will require work and that the work is worth it when we have God's glory and praise in mind. Many give up when the relationship requires work or when we place ourselves at the center instead of God's calling. When we place ourselves as the purpose of relationships, we often decide the dividend yield is not worth the investment. Is there a relationship you should put more work and effort into?

"Be humble, gentle, patient, and forbearing in love." Even before Paul mentions specific actions, he describes four key character qualities that are sometimes the opposite of what drives our relationships.

1. Humility: This quality enables us to see our own sin before we focus on the sin and weakness of another. Do you hold others to a higher standard than you do yourself?
2. Gentleness: A gentle person is not weak but someone who uses his strength to empower others. A gentle person can use strength without damaging those he is trying to help. Do people regularly feel bruised in their relationship with you?
3. Patience: This quality places others' needs higher than or at the same level as our own. We don't come with a self-centered agenda.

4. Forbearance: A forbearing person is a person who is humble, gentle, and patient even when provoked. Do you love people with limits that are driven by your own perceived needs or interests? Do others feel as if they must always return a favor to keep you happy with them?

Because we have received grace, we are to give grace to others in our relationships. Often, a structure of law, offense, and punishment governs relationships. For example: I have a set of rules you must abide by, I watch to make sure you follow these rules, and I am justified to mete out some form of punishment if you do not. This is a flagrant contradiction of the gospel! God's grace and favor in our lives should reflect his glory and show in our relationships.

"There is one Spirit, one Lord, and one Father." The basis of our unity is the unity of the Trinity, not our ability to get along. We get along because Father, Spirit, and Son have allowed us to do so.

Can you give ways in which God is humble, patient, gentle, and forbearing?

An Appreciation of Diversity

How often do we see diversity as a hindrance to good relationships and God's purposes?

Read Ephesians 4:7–16.

Because it is grounded in the Trinity, our unity also allows us to celebrate our diversity in the body of Christ. There is one God but three persons. God creates and uses our diversity to accomplish his purpose: our growth in grace. Diversity is not an obstacle but quite a significant means to this end.

"But to each one of us grace has been given as Christ apportioned it." God has created us with different gifts, different capacities for service, and different levels of maturity. All these differences are there by God's sovereign apportionment. God surrounds us with different people to promote his purpose. Do you tend to get along only with people who are most like you?

"So that the body of Christ may be built up." God wants us to mature, to be built up, and to stop acting like infants. He wants the things that ruled Christ's heart to rule ours as well. Relationships are God's tool for doing this construction. This is where the true value of relationships runs counter to what we normally think. We think things are going well only if we are getting along with others. But God says that it is also when we are not getting along with others that he is accomplishing his purposes! For example, if you quit at the first sign of fatigue when you exercise, you miss the chance to become more fit. Exercise after exhaustion is the most efficient and productive time for physical fitness. This is true of relationships as well. God has designed our relationships to function as both a diagnosis and a cure. When we are frustrated and ready to give up, God is at work revealing places where we have given in to a selfish agenda.

We enter relationships for personal pleasure, self-actualization, and fun. We want low personal cost and high self-defined returns. But God wants high personal cost and high God-defined returns.

Think of a relationship in your life that has problems because you are two very different people. Are you willing to see those differences as God's design so that you may both be built up in Christ? What may God want to teach you or reveal to you through this relationship?

Our Struggle and God's Agenda

Read Ephesians 4:17–32.

Finally, Paul lays out what relationships look like when God's purpose rules. He identifies seven tendencies of the sinful heart that are damaging to relationships, disruptive of God's purpose, and require persistent battling.

The 7 Tendencies of the Sinful Heart

1. The tendency toward self-indulgence (vv. 19–24)
    My behavior in the relationship is driven by what I want and not God's purpose.
2. The tendency toward deceit (v. 25)
    I will manipulate the truth to get what I want out of the relationship.
3. The tendency toward anger (vv. 26–27)
    I want to control the relationship by venting my anger or by holding it over you to control you.
4. The tendency toward selfishness (v. 28)
    I want to protect what I have rather than offer it to serve you.
5. The tendency toward unhelpful communication (vv. 29–30)
    Rather than use my speech to make you feel better and put you in a better position, I speak to make myself feel better and ensure that I am in the top spot.
6. The tendency toward division (v. 31)
    I give in to the temptation to view you as an adversary rather than a companion in the struggle of relationship.
7. The tendency toward an unforgiving spirit (v. 32)
    I want to make others pay for their wrongs against me.

Examine the struggles in your relationships. Which of the seven tendencies do you find yourself leaning toward most often? Ask God to help change you in this area. Share this problem with another who can help.

We are all tempted by these tendencies. We are not immune even as believers. But when we realize, by God's grace, that relationships demand hard work, we can become willing to enter the struggle rather than avoid it. We see that this is where God is present and active. We begin to run toward others rather than away and can experience the following:

*   How much wiser God's plan is for us than our plan for ourselves (vv. 19–24)
*   The life-changing power of truthfulness (v. 25)
*   The healing benefit of gentleness, patience, and love (vv. 26–27)
*   The joy of serving the needs of someone else (v. 28)

- The value of loving and wholesome communication (vv. 29–30)
- The beauty of functional unity in a relationship (v. 31)
- The freedom of practicing forgiveness (v. 32)

Closing Activity

Josh was promised a promotion, but it required moving. He and his wife, Sara, began researching the place they would have to move to. It was a nicer climate with better schools, and with the promotion they could easily afford a bigger house. Josh and Sara decided to take the promotion and moved their family of six.

Once they had settled in, they began searching for a good church to join. The first church was small and friendly but had no Sunday school for the children. The second church Sara really liked because its worship was similar to when she was growing up, but Josh did not like it. The third church they visited was big, too big for Sara to ever feel comfortable but Josh loved the worship and the preaching.

After two months of seeking, neither Sara nor Josh could agree on any one new church. Josh was angry with Sara for not being willing to try something new, and Sara was hurt that Josh wouldn't give up trivial needs for the sake of the family. After three months Sara began taking the kids to the closest church while Josh stayed home.

Decide what led to the conflict.
1. What is Josh's part in the conflict, and what is Sara's part in the conflict. What needs to occur to resolve the issues?

2. What then is God's agenda for our relationships?

Central Point

1. God has an agenda for our relationships that is often different from our own agenda.
2. Our relationships are a gift from God.
3. Relationships will require work.
4. Conflict and diversity are God's tools to mold us into his image.
5. God's grace enables us to overcome temptations to sin against another and to show gentleness, patience, humility, and forbearance.

Personal Application

1. I need to examine what I want from my relationships against what God wants for them.
2. I need to accept that relationships will take work but that they are a gift from God to mold me into his image.
3. By God's grace, I need to battle the sinful tendencies of my heart.

Relational Application

1. I need to apply God's agenda to my relationships.
2. I need to move toward relationships even when there is conflict so that God can use it to mold us into his image.

3. By God's grace I need to seek to be humble, gentle, patient, and forbearing in my relationships.

Make It Real

1. Place a check next to the statements you can agree with:

___I will seek God's agenda in my relationships instead of my own comfort and happiness.

___I will allow God to use the conflicts in my relationships to mold me into his image.

___I will take my relationships seriously as a gift from God.

___I will expect my relationships to take work.

___I will do the work necessary to maintain the unity of the Spirit.

___I will make every effort to be humble.

___I will make every effort to be gentle.

___I will make every effort to be patient.

___I will make every effort to be forbearing.

___I will accept differences not as hindrances or annoyances but as God's sovereign design.

___I will maintain my relationship to God so that his grace may help me overcome the sinful tendencies of my heart.

Place an extra check next to any statements that you feel will be especially difficult for you or next to any statements that you feel are most important for you at this time.

Share your answers with your spouse or group.

2. Next time you have conflict with someone, go to that person to resolve it but begin by agreeing to seek God's purpose from the issue instead of seeking your own (seeking to be right, seeking to be happy, seeking your own purpose).

Two Foundation Stones

Review

What is God's agenda for your relationships? Which item(s) did you place two check marks next to for lesson 3 Make It Real question 1?

Central Point and Application

Central Point: Good relationships are built on remembering who we are in God's eyes and worshipping God for who he is.

Personal Application: I can love and serve others best when I remember all I am in Christ and when I allow God to be Creator, Sovereign, and Savior.

Relational Application: I need to accept and appreciate others as they are and not take God's role in changing them or in finding my identity in them.

THE BIG QUESTION

How are your relationships affected by how you see yourself and how you see God?

Opening Thought

Even when we accept the notion that relationships will take work and are God's way of refining us, no amount of hard work will make your relationships what God intends them to be without building them on a solid foundation. We have talked about why relationships are so difficult and time consuming, but what are the foundations of a healthy, God-honoring relationship? What are the daily thoughts, desires, and habits that make relationships good? Why *do* we struggle with one person one way and with another a different way?

Consider Matt and Rob. Matt and Rob both get along well with others and have very God-honoring relationships with their wives. However, Matt and Rob's business venture, that had once been so exciting, was now fraught with conflict. Whenever Matt brought an idea about how they could use their resources for the community, Rob questioned its effectiveness in allowing the business to succeed. Matt, wanting Rob's respect and acceptance, became bitter. Or whenever Rob, wanting to be efficient, made even the smallest decision without Matt, Matt became irrational and angry. As a result they had a terrible time making decisions; and though they wanted the partnership to work and tried hard to work through the issues as they felt God wanted them to do, they never seemed to get past the disagreements and hurts. Their partnership felt like a never-ending battle.

The Two Foundation Stones

We can mistakenly think that our relationships are difficult because, like a child learning to walk, we simply lack the skills and experience not to fall. This may be true in part, but the greater problem is the foundation we are walking on. This foundation is not what we do or say. It begins in the heart (remember, the greatest problem is inside us)—the source of the thoughts to build healthy, God-honoring relationships if our heart's foundation is solid; based on God's truth, design, and purpose for us. Good relationships are always built on the foundation stones of *identity* and *worship*.

When we talk about identity, we are talking about how we define ourselves—the talents, qualities, experiences, achievements, goals, beliefs, relationships, and dreams we as individuals use to say, "This is who I am." When we talk about worship, we are talking about the things we live for—the desires, goals, treasures, purposes, values, or cravings that control our hearts. God wants, and deserves, to be the defining center of both these things. Furthermore, these foundational issues of identity and worship are an inescapable part of our nature as human beings. What we believe and do about these two things will shape the way we live with the people God has placed in our lives. When we live out of a biblical sense of who we are (identity) and rest on who God is (worship), we will be able to build healthy relationships.

Remembering Who You Are

We all try to make sense out of life by telling ourselves who we are. We all have an "I am _____, therefore I can _____" way of living. The identity we assign ourselves will always affect the way we respond to others. For example, if I tell myself that I am smarter than you, it will be difficult for me to listen when you give advice. If I tell myself that I deserve your respect, I will watch to see if you are giving me what I think I deserve.

1. Can you define the identity on which Rob and Matt's relationship stood?

The Bible provides examples of people who forgot their identities and the wrong reactions that followed, as well as people who remembered their true identities and their proper reactions. In the examples below, identify (1) what true identity each person replaced, (2) the faulty identity that replaced it, and (3) the reaction and result from the false identity.

Example: Adam and Eve eating from the forbidden tree
(1) Their true identity was to be dependent on God, living within the boundaries he set for them.
(2) They made themselves independent of God and deserving of more than God gave them.
(3) The reaction was to disobey God and eat what was forbidden, resulting in sin and separation from God.

- Sarah and Abraham having a surrogate son
(1)

(2)

(3)

- Peter separating himself from the Gentiles (Gal. 2:11–14)
(1)

(2)

(3)

Identify the identity each person remembered and held onto and the result.

- Moses leading people out of Egypt
  (1)

  (2)

  (3)

- David facing Goliath
  (1)

  (2)

  (3)

- Paul and Silas in prison
  (1)

  (2)

  (3)

Who we tell ourselves we are has quite a powerful impact on the way we deal with the big and small issues of daily life. Where we find our identity will have everything to do with how we respond to the difficult work of relationships. Either we get our identity vertically, out of our sense of who God is and who he has made us in Christ, or we will seek to get our identity horizontally, out of our circumstances, relationships, and successes. Much of the disappointment and heartache we experience is the result of finding our identity in others and attempting to get from relationships what we already have in Christ. In almost thirty years of counseling, I have talked with countless women in difficult marriages who said, "All I ever wanted was for my husband to make me happy." My first thought is invariably, *Well, then, he's cooked!*

No human being was ever meant to be the source of personal joy and contentment for someone else. And surely, no sinner is ever going to be able to pull that off day after day in the all-encompassing relationship of marriage! Our spouse, our friends, and our children cannot be the sources of our identity. If we seek our identity from others, we will watch them too closely, listen too intently, and need them too fundamentally. We will ride the roller coaster of their best and worst moments; we will become acutely aware of their weaknesses and failures; we will become overly critical, frustrated, disappointed, hopeless, and angry because they have failed to deliver the identity we seek. As a result we will be left with damaged relationships filled with hurt, frustration, and anger. On the other hand, when we remember that Christ has given us everything we need to be the people he has designed us to be, we are free to serve and love others. We are free to be humble, patient, gentle, and forbearing.

2. Is there evidence that you are looking to your relationships to give you things you have already been given in Christ? What symptoms can you identify (anger, frustration, fear, disappointment, hurt, hopelessness, etc.)?

Remembering Who God Is

Just as we all look for identity, we also are all worshippers. But we are not talking about worship as a formal religious activity but rather as an identity—what it is that controls our hearts. Our hearts are always under the control of something and whatever controls our hearts controls our behavior.

Read Matthew 6:19–24.

Jesus says what we worship (our treasure) is what will control us (where our heart will be). We cannot serve two masters—we will serve what we value most. This has an interesting application for relationships. Often when we value something other than pleasing God, we will end up valuing and serving ourselves; but when we value God, we will serve and love others. Here are three ways that our worship of God affects our relationships with others:

1. Read Psalm 139:13–16. Worshipping God as Creator

    a. If you have been fearfully and wonderfully made, what does that mean in how you see and treat others?

    b. If you worship God as the Creator, what is your role in trying to change others?

Although most of us have affirmed that God is the Creator of all things, it is quite easy to worship him as Creator on Sunday and then curse his work during the week. We do this when we are dissatisfied with the way God has made the people we relate to each day. In fact, we often ascend his throne and do all we can to recreate others in our *own* image!

Have you ever tried to recreate someone in your own likeness? Without realizing it, that is what Matt and Rob were doing to each other. Rob was a visionary who was trying to turn his detail-oriented partner into a dreamer. Matt was an administrator who was trying to recreate Rob into his own image (for the sake of the company, of course!). If you're not affirming the glory of God in the way he made another (including all the ways someone is different from you), you will be frustrated with who the other person is and tempted to remake them in some way. If I am ever going to value who you are and benefit from our differences, I must look at you and see the wisdom of the Creator.

2. Read Acts 17:26. Worshipping God as Sovereign

If it is God who has determined our backgrounds, how should we see and treat the differences between us?

God has specifically and personally determined the details of each of our lives. When I look at you I need to see God's hand perfectly writing your story. The person you are and the responses you make to life have been shaped by his sovereign choices and your responses to the story he has written for you.

He determined that you would be part of the customs and culture of a certain ethnic group. He planned that you would be shaped by living in a certain geological setting. He determined that you would live in a particular family, with all of its powerfully influential values and rules, spoken and unspoken.

He also determined that you would be involved in relationships and situations outside your home that would have a powerful influence on everything you do. A relationship is the intersection of the stories of two people. The problem is that an awful lot of carnage takes place at this intersection.

If I fail to honor God's sovereignty in the influences he has placed in your life and the way those influences have shaped you, I will attempt to take God's place and clone you into my image. I will tend to think my way is better than your way.

Are you frustrated with someone in your life? Are you trying to reshape that person to fit into your personal preferences?

3. Read Romans 3:22–24. Worshipping God as Savior
   Though God has made us all unique, we are exactly the same in
   two ways.

   According to this passage what are the two ways we are the same?

Worshipping God as Savior means that we acknowledge that we
are sinners in relationships with other sinners. We remember that
others are still in the middle of God's work of redemption—as we
are—and that he is faithfully working in others at the best time
and in the best way possible. None of us gets to be in relationships with finished persons. When we forget that we are sinners
saved by grace, we become self-righteous, impatient, critical, and
judgmental. We give in to the temptation to play God and try to
change others in ways only God can.

When we fail to worship God as Savior, we are too casual
about our sin and too focused on others'. Our relationships are
often harmed when we try to atone for our own sins while condemning others for theirs. When we are sinned against, we will be
impacted by the weaknesses and failures of others, but we need to
allow God to use us as instruments in his redemptive hands rather
than seek to make changes in the other people whom only God
can change.

Are you trying to do work in someone's life that only the
Savior can do?

Closing Activity

Worship.

Central Point

1. Good relationships are built on a true identity and true worship.
2. I am free to love and serve others when I focus on what I have already been given in Christ (identity).
3. I can best accept and appreciate others when I worship God as Creator, Sovereign, and Savior.

Personal Application

1. I need to examine where I get my identity.
2. I have everything I need in Christ.
3. I need to examine what my treasure really is.
4. I need to let God be God and not try to do his work.

Relational Application

1. I need to stop looking for what I think I need from others.
2. I need to give people time to change and accept and appreciate them as God's workmanship.
3. I need to accept that God is in control of who people are and allow *him* to work as he sees best.

Make It Real

1. Make a search of Scripture for statements that describe your identity in Christ. (Some examples are Eph. 1–3; 1 Pet. 2:9–12; 1 John 3:1–3.) Select one you think you often forget, and write it out on a note card.

   For Example:
   "I am an ambassador for God"
   or "There is therefore no condemnation."

   Place the card where you will see it or make it your screen saver.

2. Be honest, what have you been wanting to get from your relationships that you already have in Christ? Are you willing to look to Jesus for what you need?

3. Keep being honest, what have you been trying to change in another person that can only be changed by God? Are you willing to let God be in control of the other person?

4. Examine any problems you may be experiencing in relationships, and try to identify whether you are standing on a false identity or whether you are worshipping yourself instead of God. Confess your sin to God and to the other person.

Relationships and Communication

Review

Share with the group verses you found that describe our identity in Christ.

What is the problem in any relationship?

What are the two foundation stones upon which healthy relationships are built?

Central Point and Application

Central Point: As Christ's ambassadors, we represent him every time we speak.

Personal Application: I need to seek God's grace in how I communicate with others and choose to be his ambassador.

Relational Application: As Christ's ambassador, I need to speak in a way that is helpful to those God has placed me in relationship with.

THE BIG QUESTION
Will you choose to speak as an ambassador of Christ?

Opening Activity

Game of Ambassadors

A Radical Commitment to the Call of Christ

Read 2 Corinthians 5:20.

1. What job description does Paul assign us?

2. How is that job description significant in our relationship with God?

    a. In our communication with others?

As ambassadors, we do one thing—represent Christ. As ambassadors, it is our job to incarnate a king who is not present. The king's interests will direct every word we speak. Therefore, as ambassadors, what we say must be driven by what God is seeking to accomplish in us and in other people.

3. According to 2 Corinthians 5:20, what is God trying to accomplish?

God is working in every situation and in every relationship to reclaim our wandering hearts, and he calls us to speak in a way that has this reconciliation in view. Unfortunately, we lose sight of reconciliation in many ways: When we flatter friends because we want them to like us. When we trim the truth to avoid a conflict. When we yell at our children about their messy rooms. When winning arguments is all we care about. When we indulge in gossip. When we are better at pointing out wrong than asking for forgiveness. When we use words to hurt others rather than help them. When our communication stays resolutely impersonal. When our words make us the center of attention.

Here is the point: our words are always in pursuit of some kind of kingdom. We are either speaking as mini-kings, seeking to establish our will in our relationships and circumstances, or we are speaking as ambassadors, seeking to be part of what the King is doing. And when two mini-kings talk to each other, the battle of words has no end! When our words reflect the self-focused desires of our hearts rather than God's work of reconciliation, our struggle has no end. When we use words to establish our will rather than submit to God's, we plunge into difficulty. If we are ever to be helped, this is where we must start.

The vast majority of our communication takes place in the inconsequential moments of everyday life. As a result, we can view communication as ordinary and insignificant. The moments are rare when what we say will literally be life changing. However, the course of our lives is set by the ways we respond to the little moments. The character developed in a thousand little moments is what we carry into the big, important moments.

For instance, every day, we tell people what we think of them, what we want from them, and what we would like to enjoy from them. But we don't do this in grand moments of oratory. We do it in quick side comments in the bedroom as we get ready for work or at the curb as we hop into the car or in the kitchen as we grab a sandwich or over dessert at the local bistro or in the family room during a commercial. It is these moments of everyday conversation that influence the shape, quality, and direction of our relationships. Every day, our words give our relationships their tone.

There has never been a good relationship without good communication, and there has never been a bad relationship that didn't get that way in part because of something that was said. The Bible has much to say about our world of talk. The Bible does not consider this area of life ordinary or unimportant. In fact, it does the opposite. It assigns words that extraordinary value they actually deserve.

God's Perspective on Our Words

Our Words Have Power

The Message translates Proverbs 18:21 "Words kill, words give life; they're either poison or fruit—you choose."

1. How can words kill?

2. How can words give life?

Our words always have direction. They can either be constructive or destructive. Words have power. Think about your communication in the last week. Has it been more destructive or constructive? Think about a conflict you had with someone. Did you direct your words to be life giving or deadly?

Our Words Belong to the Lord

Genesis 1 makes clear God spoke the first words ever spoken. Language is not a human invention and therefore belongs to God. Language is his creation. Our ability to speak sets us apart from the animals and was given to us by God for his glory. Words are a gift calling us to live and speak in a God-focused manner. One of our greatest mistakes in communication is to take words as our own to use as we please. This is what the teenager does as he publicly mocks a friend. This is what a husband does as he criticizes his wife at dinner. This is what friends do as they gossip on the phone. This is what the demanding, critical parent does. They are all stealing God's glory by treating words as their own creation.

The World of Talk Is a World of Trouble

If you are honest, you have to admit that your relationships have been troubled by words as much as they have been helped. Who can honestly say that all his words are well intentioned and appropriately spoken? Who has not hurt someone with words or used words in a selfish manner? Who has not turned the gift of language into a weapon of anger? Read James 3:2b.

1. What does James indicate about our words?

Word Problems Are Heart Problems
Read Luke 6:45.

1. According to Jesus, our words come from where?

2. What then is the real problem, when our words create conflict?

Have you ever said, "Oops, I didn't mean to say that"? Often it would be more accurate to say, "I'm sorry I said what I meant"! The real problem with our communication is *what* we *want* to say and *why* we *want* to say it. The problem actually begins before the words are even spoken. Christ says the heart shapes the *what* and the *why*. Therefore, if we hope to transform the way we talk to one another, the heart must change first.

Talking Like an Ambassador

What does it mean to communicate like an ambassador? Does it mean that we quote Scripture incessantly or constantly point out the sin in others? Does it mean we can never talk about sports or the weather? What about the daily need to discuss the details of life—schedules, responsibilities, problems, and plans—with people?

Read Ephesians 4:29–30.

Here is a practical model of ambassadorial communication. Speaking as an ambassador is not about using biblical words; it's about speaking with a biblical agenda.

Speaking with a Biblical Agenda

If we want our words to reflect what God wants more than what we want, we should consider three things:

1. Consider the person ("only what is helpful for building others up")
   Wholesome communication is others-centered. When our words are shaped more by our interests than others', they lose their shelter from difficulty. Paul says we should never say anything that is not helpful for others. Because God is focused on remaking us into his image, we should speak in a way that builds people up as well. We are his ambassadors. We now have a redemptive agenda for talking about everything. We want all of our talk to be redemptively constructive, from the most mundane details to the huge life decisions. As ambassadors, we never want our words to be obstacles to what the King is doing. Our words must always be others-centered.

2. Consider the problem ("according to their needs")
   Ambassadors who are always centered on others also must always be asking, "What is the problem at this moment?" Before we speak, we must think about what *others* are struggling with and what *others* most need. Do they need encouragement, comfort, hope, direction, wisdom, courage, rebuke, warning, forgiveness, patience, teaching, correction, thanks, a job description, or

something else? Our words are shaped by their needs. An ambassador's words always address the person's true need of the moment.
3.   Consider the process ("that it may benefit those who listen") This means that we focus on the best way to say what needs to be said. Ambassadorial communication is not only about the content of our words but the manner in which they are spoken. Often we choose to say the right thing at the wrong time or in the wrong way. But the communication process needs to benefit the person as much as the content of the words. Confronting a teenager five minutes before she leaves for school is not helpful, even if the content is accurate. Rebuking a friend for an offense in front of others is not helpful. Asking your husband to consider how you hurt him as he is trying to get to sleep is not helpful. An ambassador seeks to speak the right thing in the best way.

Will you be Christ's ambassador to those he places you in relationship with? Our relationships have been designed as workrooms for redemption, not shelters for human happiness. Paul's practical model to guide our words ends with something very interesting: "Do not grieve the Holy Spirit." Not only do our self-centered, unhelpful and untimely words hurt and grieve other people; they also grieve the Lord.

Closing Activity: Giving Encouragement

At times, speaking as Christ's ambassador means confronting another about sin. Of course, how we confront is just as important. For this activity, we only want to encourage. Sit across from a partner or in a small group and tell that person what God would want him or her to know or to remember. Some ideas could include telling him how special he is to God, the way you see God use him in the lives of others or in your own life, the gifts you see God has given her, the hope she has in Christ, the strengths of her personality and background, and so on.

Central Point
1. Words are significant.
2. Our words belong to God.
3. The problem we have with words is really a problem we have in our heart.

Personal Application

1. If I want God's will in my relationships, I need to seriously consider the words I use and how I speak them.
2. I need to submit my will to God's so that the words that overflow from my heart are not self-seeking.
3. I need to take seriously my role as Christ's ambassador and represent him in what I say.

Relational Application

1. I need to see my relationships as opportunities for God to use me in the life of another as his ambassador.
2. I need to consider the other person's interest when I speak.
3. I need to consider what the other person is struggling with when I speak.
4. I need to consider the best way to say the right thing.

Making It Real

1. Think of a time when you found it difficult to use words in a helpful way. Where was your focus? What would you have done had you remembered or realized that you were God's ambassador at that moment for the benefit of the other person?

2. Describe your greatest problem with words. Angry, sarcastic, defensive, demeaning, negative, critical, superficial, offensive, mean, and so forth. What is the thinking in your heart from which this attitude or tone overflows?

3. Memorize Ephesians 4:29–30.

Conflict

Review/Opening Activity

For the better part of five years, Ashley and Hannah had worked side by side in campus ministry. They loved what they did, and they loved doing it together. But Hannah had been slowly seeking to undermine Ashley's relationship with students. She wanted to be seen as the one who was more capable and in charge. To put it bluntly, she wanted the students to like and admire her more than Ashley. Now Ashley felt things had gotten out of control. Once again her friend had just hurt her, so she made an appointment to meet with Hannah to speak her mind.

Ashley began the meeting accusing Hannah of talking about her negatively to some students. "I can't believe you talk that way behind my back! I have never done that to you, and I never would." Ashley's hurt had boiled over into anger and accusation.

Hannah denied everything. "I can't believe you would accuse me of saying those things to other people. I thought our friendship was stronger than that. How come you have held this in for five years? Why didn't you just come to me earlier?"

As the two talked, the origin of the problem began to emerge. While talking to someone who did not care for Ashley, Hannah had made a casual comment about how "task-oriented" Ashley could be. She said it was a real pain sometimes to live with her. This remark took on a life of its own when the person repeated it to others with her own embellishments. Eventually the word found its way back to Ashley. By then it sounded as if Hannah saw her friend as a task-oriented demon who just used people to accomplish her ministry goals.

It's inevitable. If we live with other sinners, we will have conflict. The closer we are to others, the more potential there is for conflict.

1. Evaluate Hannah and Ashley's conflict. What is the root of the problem? (Don't forget, our problem with words is first a heart problem.)

2. What will restore the relationship?

Central Point and Application

Central Point: Relationships inevitably bring conflict but also growth.

Personal Application: I need to face conflict and be willing to identify the selfish desires of my heart that lead to conflict.

Relational Application: I need to commit to working through conflict for the good of the relationship, be willing to accept and confess my sin, and consider the needs of the other person.

THE BIG QUESTION
What are the sinful desires that lead to conflict?

Facing Conflicts Head On

Relationships are costly but so is avoiding them. If we choose to avoid relationships and the conflicts that arise, we will minimize the conflict in our lives, but we will also miss out on God's redemptive work in our lives.

Remember, Father, Son, and Spirit were torn apart when Jesus died so that we might embrace rather than exclude one another. God wants to make us more like Christ, and he wants to use others to make that happen. We must be willing to face conflict and deal with it in a God-centered way.

The Cause and Cure of Ungodly Conflict

Why can't at least one relationship in our lives come with a "no conflict" label attached to it? Some people think that is what marriage is for, and these people are in for a surprise! In reality, marriage is the most likely place for conflict, but close relationships such as marriage are also the most likely places for supernatural change to occur.

If we have a problem, conflict is a good one to have. Why? Because conflict is a problem the Bible addresses quite directly. We don't have to be expert Bible scholars to get help here. All we need is a heart that is ready and willing to hear the answer.

Read James 4:1–10.

1. According to this passage in James, why do we fight with one another?

James says the root of conflict is within *us*. Often our typical response to conflict is to point the finger at the other person. We say things such as, "I did that because you . . ." or "I wouldn't be so angry if you wouldn't . . . ." We like to justify our response because the other person has done something annoying, frustrating, or even downright sinful. But James is clear; conflict arises from the desires that battle within us. The word *desire* that James uses here is a word that would be better translated as "selfish desire." All desires are not wrong, but a selfish desire is.

Conflict broke out between my wife and me in our kitchen. I was putting the dishes away, and she was cooking dinner. We both got into each other's way and then got sarcastic with each other. I said, "I would hate to get in your way while I load the dishwasher!" She replied, "I would hate to get in your way while I cook dinner!"

What was going on? I had a desire to accomplish a task and was feeling rather self-righteous about what a sacrificial husband I was. My wife also had a desire to accomplish a task and was feeling self-righteous about what a sacrificial wife and mother she was. Both of our desires quickly turned from good to selfish. I wanted to serve, but it had to be on my terms and on my time schedule. My wife wanted to serve, but she wanted to do it without any distractions. The selfishness showed itself in our self-righteous comments. We both wanted to be recognized for our service, and when that did not happen, we had conflict. We divorced our service from God's glory and the other's good and turned it into self-service.

Think of a recent conflict you had with someone. Identify the desire in your heart that led to the conflict by taking a look at the desires below. They are not sinful, in and of themselves, until they become selfish desires. They also can be revealed by what we fear because often what we fear is not getting what we want. Do you identify with any of these temptations? Were one of these desires in your heart during your last conflict?

- Comfort: I want, must have, and deserve to be comfortable, and you'd better not get in the way of me getting it! (I fear hard work and sacrifice.)
- Pleasure: I want, must have, and deserve to feel good, and you'd better make me feel that way! (I fear pain.)

- Recognition: I want, must have, and deserve to be recognized, or I will be devastated. (I fear being overlooked or unnoticed.)
- Power: I want, must have, and deserve power, and you'd better do what I say! (I fear being told what to do.)
- Control: I want, must have, and deserve control, and you will feel the brunt of my disappointment if you mess up my tidy little universe! (I fear unpredictability and the unknown.)
- Acceptance: I want, must have, and deserve acceptance, and you are responsible for giving it to me. (I fear rejection.)

2. Which of these desires has become more important to you than your relationship to God?

3. Which of these desires tends to be the one(s) that most often leads to conflict in your life?

4. In James 4:4, what does it mean to be a "friend of the world"?

Ashley and Hannah had made recognition and reputation more important than God's glory and grace. They had made a piece of creation their best friend and primary focus.

5. Do you find anything encouraging in James 4:4?

Next time you experience ungodly irritation with a friend, spouse, coworker, or child, ask yourself, "What is more important to me right now than God's glory?"

What Does God Do to People Who Forsake Him for Something Else?

Consider a married couple where one of the partners has a one-night stand. This person has betrayed the one to whom he is supposed to be most committed. He has shared with another an intimacy that only the spouse can rightly claim. What would you expect the offended spouse to do? Would you expect that person to act as though nothing has happened? What if the offended spouse said, "Oh, that's okay"? Wouldn't you wonder whether that person really cared about the relationship? If the offended person was even slightly invested in the marriage, you would expect to see some jealousy and anger over infidelity, wouldn't you?

So it is with God.

Read James 4:5–6.

When we wander from God, the Spirit he has poured out on us and who now lives in us becomes quite concerned and envious. A better way to translate the words *envious* or *jealous* is the word *zealous*. Like the person who is unfaithful, God is zealous to do whatever it takes to regain the affection of our hearts. He doesn't do this because he needs us; he does this because he loves us. When he pursues us and we humble ourselves and return to him, he pours out even more grace!

1. Based on what we have learned so far, what do you think God uses to regain our affections?

God uses the difficulties in relationships to allow us to see what we typically live for besides him. God used Ashley and Hannah in each other's lives to help them grow in repentance and faith.

Who is God using in your life right now? Do you see that your wise, sovereign, and gracious Redeemer was acting on your behalf when he placed this person in your life? If so, you are growing in your ability to engage in conflict in godly ways. Remember, you can't avoid conflict, but it can be a place where amazing growth takes place!

Once We Are Rescued, What Should We Do?
Read James 4:7–10.

Seeing God's redeeming love should lead us to grow in the joy of daily repentance and faith. Seeing, admitting, confessing, and forsaking sin (repentance) in combination with seeing, acknowledging, and adoring Christ (faith) is the only dynamic that can change a war-maker into a peacemaker. We are called to resist Satan's schemes to use parts of creation to entice our still-sinful hearts. We are commanded to humble ourselves and submit ourselves to God. Through humility and crying out to God for help, our hearts will be changed and purified, and our behavior will change as well.

In the kitchen that night, my wife and I experienced God's grace and moved in a different direction after our disagreement. Rather than continuing to point the finger and fight for our own glory, self-protection, and self-love, we confessed our sin, asked for forgiveness, and continued working together. You may be wondering why I have shared such a minor incident. It's because if we don't grow in these little moments, we won't grow when the more difficult times come, such as needing to love an enemy.

Let's Get Practical

To apply what James 4 teaches, we have to begin with relationships built on commitment and love. Within those relationships we can start to form habits that can be practiced later on in tougher moments of conflict. What then does it look like to engage in godly conflict in the heat of the moment?

Understand that conflict is one way God works in our lives. In fact, God himself entered into conflict when he humbly came as a man to fight on our behalf against the ravages of sin. He calls us to imitate him as we engage in conflict with others. Godly conflict is an act of compassion.

Identify what drives ungodly conflict in our lives. What tends to lure our loyalty and affection away from God? Be specific and don't be surprised if each instance of ungodly conflict reveals a different idol, whether it be acceptance, power, control, recognition, pleasure, or being right.

Recognize our default strategy in conflict. Most of us have a default strategy we use to get what we want. Do we love to fight because we have to be right? Do we avoid conflict because we don't want people to disapprove of us? Do we avoid conflict because we don't like discomfort?

Engage in specific and intelligent spiritual warfare. When we see what we typically live for and how we try to get it, we can start to grow in repentance and faith. We want to be brutally honest about our sin, but we also want to be ardently hopeful about what Christ has done for us on the cross. We want to remember that because we have the Holy Spirit, we already have the resources available to fight against ungodly conflict.

Consider the other person.

Read 1 Thessalonians 5:14–18.

1. What different actions does Paul say we should consider when considering the other person?

2. What does Paul say we should always do when we consider another person?

As our hearts are reclaimed by the grace of God, as individuals we should ask questions about what it will look like to engage in godly conflict. Do I need to pursue someone and confront him? Do I need to be patient and encourage him? Do I need to overlook an offense? What sins and weaknesses in the other person do I need to consider? Paul says there are different ways to confront, based on what the person needs and what will build him up.

Make a plan to approach the person. If we think patience has run its course and we need to address an issue, approach the person in this way:

- Own whatever personal sin we have brought to the situation. Only do this if you have sin to own—sometimes you will; sometimes you won't. Most of the time we do bring sin into the situation, so don't be afraid to admit where you have not loved well, even if your sin was your response to the other's sin. Our confidence in Christ's righteousness (and not our own) is the only thing that will enable us to do this!
- Agree together that we want God's will. This can take the focus off of ourselves and remind us that God wants to use the conflict for our growth. It also gives us both the same focus as we move forward.
- Name the problem. We may need to address more than one problem. Be specific so that we are both dealing with the same problem. Deal with one problem at a time!
- Explore possible solutions. Stay focused on the problem, and come with a desire to deal with it. Suggest possible alternative solutions, and choose one to implement.
- Implement the agreed upon solution. Be specific and determine what it will look like.

- Evaluate our implementation. Make a commitment to get together again and evaluate how the solution is working. Such a commitment is a form of accountability. It communicates a deep commitment to the relationship.
- If we get stuck and things don't improve, be willing to get outside help. Together we should choose a person we believe will respect both sides of the conflict.

No one ever said that conflict would be fun, but the Christian life is not always fun. That is not the most important thing to God. He is committed to something much bigger. His kingdom plan involves a total restoration of what he has made. He will settle for nothing less in his creation than to see that all things ultimately bring him glory. He will be the center of everything at the end of the age, and when that happens, we will be most satisfied. Right now, he is using conflict to work out this comprehensive plan in us. Take heart, for he is present in our struggles and he is fighting on our behalf!

C. S. Lewis wrote:

> . . . we must not be surprised if we are in for a rough time. When a man turns to Christ and seems to be getting on pretty well (in the sense that some of his habits are now corrected), he often feels that it would now be natural if things went fairly smoothly. When troubles come along—illnesses, money troubles, new kinds of temptation—he is disappointed. These things, he feels, might have been necessary to rouse him and make him repent in his bad old days; but why now? Because God is forcing him on, or up, to a higher level: putting him in situations where he will have to be very much braver, or more patient, or more loving, than he ever dreamed of being before. It seems to us all unnecessary, but that is because we have not yet had the slightest notion of the tremendous thing he means to make of us.
>
> I find I must borrow yet another parable from George MacDonald. Imagine yourself as a house. God comes in to rebuild that house. At first, perhaps, you can understand what he is doing. He is getting the drains right and stopping

the leaks in the roof and so on: you knew that those jobs needed doing and so you are not surprised. But presently he starts knocking the house about in a way that hurts abominably and does not seem to make sense. What on earth is he up to? The explanation is that he is building quite a different house from the one you thought of—throwing out a new wing here, putting on an extra floor there, running up towers, making courtyards. You thought you were going to be made into a decent little cottage: but he is building a palace. He intends to come and live in it himself.[1]

Closing Activity

It began as a great family vacation. Troy, Angela, and their two boys were staying the week at the beach with Troy's parents. Troy's parents had rented a house and invited his family to join them for a week. Often, Troy's mother prepared breakfast for everyone and cleaned up.

This morning she also made breakfast but started to get ready for the beach soon after. Troy and Angela, still finishing their meal, had excused their boys to also get ready. Angela stands and says she is going to get ready and, because she tends to take a much longer time to get ready than Troy, asks Troy if he would clear the table. Troy says he will; Angela wanders back to their room.

Troy finishes eating and then sits down on the sofa with a book. Minutes later, Angela comes out of the room, sees Troy on the couch, the dishes still on the kitchen table, and incredulously asks, "What are you doing?!" Troy responds, "What?" as if he doesn't know what she means even though he knows exactly why Angela is getting upset. He figures that if he acts like he doesn't know what the problem is, then it will make it look as if *she* is the source of the problem.

Sensing what Troy is trying to do, Angela answers, "You said you would clear the dishes, that's what," in such a way to ensure that he knows it isn't even the dishes left out that is the problem as much as it is his complete stupidity and laziness.

"I know, and I will. I just sat down for a second; I can clear them later."

---

1. C. S. Lewis, *Mere Christianity* (New York: Macmillan, 1943), 174.

"No, Troy, you need to do it now, or your mom will end up doing it. Why can't you help out for once?"

"Well, if it's that important to you, why didn't you do it?" Troy asks, although he knows it is a bad question to ask because naturally she will have a good answer. So, sensing the tide has shifted against him, Troy adds, "You're making this into a big deal. We're on vacation, so why can't you just let everyone enjoy themselves?"

Angela, looking as if she is about to cry, turns abruptly, walks back to their room, and slams the door. "He better come make this right," she tells herself.

Troy, flopping back onto the sofa tells himself, "I'm not giving her the satisfaction of me going back there."

1. Beginning at this point, what do Troy and Angela need to think about and then do to resolve the conflict and restore the relationship? Try coming up with an answer without looking back at the notes from this lesson, and then look back and make any additions or revisions.

Central Point

1. Relationships inevitably bring conflict.
2. God chooses to use conflict to defeat sin in us and make us more like Christ.
3. Christ is present to help us in the midst of conflict and lift us up when we humble ourselves.

Personal Application

1. I need to face conflict and not avoid it.
2. I need to identify the selfish desires of my heart that lead to conflict.
3. I need to keep God and his glory first in my life.

Relational Application

1. I need to commit to working through conflict for the good of the relationship.
2. I need to accept and confess my sin to the other person.
3. I need to consider the needs of the other person.

Make It Real

1. Sit down with someone you are in close relationship with (spouse, child, work partner, etc.), ask that person the following questions, and write down his or her answers.

When we get into a conflict, what do you most often need from me? (to listen, to talk, to confess, to ask questions, encouragement, patience, etc.)

What is your greatest fear? (the unknown, sacrifice, pain, rejection, loss of control, change, being unrecognized, etc.)

What do you feel we need to change in how we resolve and communicate through conflict?

2. Place a check next to the statements that tend to define you.

    ___ I often try to avoid conflict even when I feel I should say something.
    ___ I usually do not look for my own sin.
    ___ I rarely confess my sin.
    ___ I often am quicker to fulfill my needs than consider the needs of the other person.
    ___ I have not been as willing as I should be for God to use conflict to mold me into his image.
    ___ I often feel hopeless or disappointed in the midst of conflict.
    ___ I expected my closest relationships to be conflict-free.
    ___ When I am in conflict with another, my greatest desire is often to be proven right.

Write a commitment to God below. What are you willing to change and work on so that you might honor God with your times of conflict?

Forgiveness: Absorbing the Cost

Review

Congratulations! You are halfway through the study. Share with the group what you have learned and benefited from so far. Have you experienced a change in your relationships? What has God been working on in your own heart?

Central Point and Application

Central Point: As a community of forgiven people, we are called to practice forgiveness.

Personal Application: I need to remember the debt Jesus absorbed on my behalf so that I might be forgiven.

Relational Application: I need to forgive others just as Christ has forgiven me.

THE BIG QUESTION

Will you seek and grant forgiveness as God calls you to do?

Opening Activity

Can you identify with any of these scenarios?

- Grace felt betrayed, and she had been. Her husband John had met someone on the Internet six months ago; they had been having an affair for the past three. Grace found out when she used John's user name to log onto their computer. When she saw the string of instant messages, she was devastated. What was she going to do? She fluctuated between wanting revenge and blaming herself.

- A family member abused Heather in her early teens. She was in college now, living under a cloud of guilt. She kept her hair long because it covered her face; it felt like a form of protection. Like Grace, she fluctuated between guilt and revenge.

- Andy and Melissa had been married for twenty years. Their marriage was strong and growing. But a few days ago Melissa had gotten irritated when Andy came home from work late. She said something sarcastic to him—she couldn't even remember what. But Andy's response was angry, self-justifying, and critical. Days later, the tension was still there. Sin had crept up on them and created a barrier between them.

- Bill loved his children and wanted them to grow up to be godly adults. They were teenagers now, developing a mind of their own. One day, Bill's son Michael came in from the backyard and slammed the door. He was upset that his brother had reneged on a promise to play basketball. Bill immediately got up and yelled at Michael for being so angry. "You have a problem, son, and I'm not going to tolerate it anymore. Your anger is out of control! Go back outside and cool down!" When Michael heard his father yell, he yelled back, turned around, and ran out the door.

C. S. Lewis wrote:

> To forgive the incessant provocations of daily life—to keep on forgiving the bossy mother-in-law, the bullying husband, the nagging wife, the selfish daughter, the deceitful son—how can we do it? Only, I think, by remembering where we stand, by meaning our words when we say in our prayers each night, "Forgive us our trespasses as we forgive those that trespass against us." We are offered forgiveness on no other terms. To refuse it is to refuse God's mercy for us. There is no hint of exceptions and God means what he says.

The Lord's Prayer commands us to pray, "Forgive our trespasses as we forgive our debtors" right after it instructs us to pray for daily bread. Practicing forgiveness is something we must do daily in the same way we ask for the daily provision of food. It is a part of everyday life, not something reserved for life's "big" sins and events, and yet forgiveness is one of the most poorly practiced activities in the Christian community—if it is practiced at all. I know this from pastoral and personal experience.

I had been a Christian for nearly twenty years and married for nearly ten before I understood what it meant to practice forgiveness with my wife! I also have met with hundreds of couples seeking help in their marriages. One of the most common problems is the giving and receiving of forgiveness. I have met couples who have been married for twenty years, yet neither spouse has truly ever admitted sin and asked for forgiveness. How can this be?

The Bible is the story of a God who forgives, calling those who have been forgiven to be forgiving people. Yet so little of the forgiveness that has been received translates into forgiveness being offered. We need help!

Define *forgiveness.*

1. What can cause forgiving to be so difficult?

What Does It Mean to Forgive?

Read Matthew 18:21–35.

Forgiveness Involves Canceling a Debt

The metaphor of debt cancelation clearly defines the nature of forgiveness. The merciful king absorbed a $100,000 debt that was owed to him. When we forgive someone, we also cancel a debt. But, more specifically, we make a conscious choice to absorb the cost ourselves. We choose not to make the offender pay for the offense. Also, by forfeiting our right to collect, we make at least three promises.

1. We promise to never bring up the debt as leverage. When we forgive, we are saying that we will not make the offenders pay by reminding them of what they have done (what they owe) in an effort to control them. This does not mean that we can't discuss it and seek to deal with the offense in a redemptive way. This is where the godly conflict we discussed earlier comes into play.

2. We promise to never bring up the offense to others and slander the persons who sinned against us. This does not mean we cannot seek the advice and counsel of others as we work through the issue, but it does mean that we will not slander the person under the guise of getting outside advice. We also will not gossip about what the person has done to us.

3. We promise to not dwell on the offense ourselves. One of the biggest challenges when someone sins against us is to not replay the offense over and over again in our mind.

If we break one of these promises than we have not fully forgiven; we have not truly canceled the debt. Our desire to make the person pay outweighs our desire to forgive.

1. How well do you truly forgive? Do you ever struggle with breaking one of these promises? Do you struggle with truly absorbing the cost of forgiveness?

Forgiveness Is Costly, but Not Forgiving Is More Costly

No matter how we spin it, forgiveness is costly; canceling a debt and absorbing the cost is going to hurt. It is this pain that often makes true forgiveness so difficult, but we must be made aware that there is a greater cost to not forgiving!

1. What is the lesson and warning Jesus makes from the parable?

An abiding unwillingness to forgive will cost us eternally. It will also make us bitter and unloving people, and we will eventually damage all our relationships.

A failure to forgive will change us. The unmerciful servant, who before the king was the victim of his own negligence, turns into a victimizer by his own unwarranted bitterness and anger. Notice what he does to the other servant: he "seized him by the throat" and had him thrown in jail. It feels so natural to make someone pay, but a sense of justice quickly goes into overdrive and turns into revenge. We may not choke anyone, but we may shut others out of our lives. Bitterness gets its foot in the door, and eventually, if the situation is not addressed and forgiveness is not granted, it takes over. And if we don't practice forgiveness on a daily basis with the little skirmishes, we'll begin to lose the battles, which will eventually cost us the war.

Forgiveness is an event and a process.

2. What is the implication of Jesus telling Peter we are to forgive "seventy times seven"?

Always the temptation exists to slip into bitterness some time in the future. Even if we have forgiven for an offense, we will be tempted to think about it the next time we see the person or the next time she sins against us. Without realizing it, we will pile that sin on top of the old sins, making it much more difficult for us to forgive; therefore, we not only need to forgive once but continue to forgive even the same sin.

Forgiveness is not forgetting. In Jeremiah 31:34, God says, "I will forgive their wickedness and will remember their sins no more." This verse, some say, is how we should forgive; that true forgiveness forgets what someone has done to us. This understanding of forgiveness creates at least two problems.

First, it is not realistic. Our minds do not function this way, and our ability to remember is powerful. In the same way, trying to forget a sin someone has committed against us will only encourage us to remember it. Completely erasing our memory is unrealistic.

Second, the passage in Jeremiah does not say that God has amnesia when he looks at you. Our omniscient God does not forget anything! The word *remember* is not a memory but a promise word, a covenant word. God is promising that when we confess our sins, "I will not treat you as your sins deserve. Instead I will forgive you." This is why forgiveness is both a past and an ongoing process into the future. It is a past promise you keep in the future. When this is done, the memory of small offenses usually dissipates. Larger offenses probably will not.

Grace will never forget about John's affair. Heather will never forget her abuse. Melissa and Andy will always be aware that they have sinned against each other. Michael will remember the times his father was sinfully angry. But each individual can still practice biblical forgiveness; they can make a promise and remain faithful to that promise over time. If Grace believes she must forget, she may be plagued with doubts about whether she has truly forgiven him, or if she believes she can forgive him once but hold onto the hurt into the future, she will become subtly bitter.

3. Answering with only a "yes" or "no," is there an offense committed against you that you still remember? When you remember, do you lean toward bitterness or practice forgiveness all over again?

Forgiveness has a vertical and a horizontal dimension.

4. Is Grace still supposed to forgive John if John does not repent?

Forgiveness does not mean peace at all costs. Matthew chapter 18 instructs us on how to deal with the sin of others. Verses 1–5 teach that life in the kingdom requires humility to confront someone gently about his sin. Verses 6–9 teach that life in the kingdom requires taking sin seriously. We can't sweep it under the rug in our own lives or in the lives of others. Verses 10–14 teach that life in the kingdom involves going after wayward people. Real love demands pursuit. And verses 15–17 teach us how to approach someone who has sinned against us.

Read Matthew 18:15–17.

The Bible never says, "Make it easy for someone to sin against you." Instead, it provides a way to deal with sin in redemptive ways. Romans 12:18 says, "If it is possible, as far as it depends on you, live at peace with everyone." Paul calls us to strive for peace, but he knows there are limits involved when we pursue someone in love. When we have reached those limits, other redemptive options are available. Our attempt to love a habitually abusive, unrepentant person sometimes involves confrontation and possibly separation. Sometimes, church leaders may need to be involved. Sometimes the state intervenes on the offended party's behalf.

Asking For and Granting Forgiveness (15 mins.)

Evaluate the following dialogue between Andy and Melissa.

> "Melissa, I am sorry you got so upset when I yelled at you. I hate it when that happens."
> "That's OK, Andy. I guess I was just tired after a long day at work." .

If a sin truly is committed, it has to be specifically acknowledged by the person who sinned. That person then needs to ask for forgiveness for the specific sin. The offended person then must choose to forgive or not forgive. If this doesn't occur in this way, at some point Melissa is going to become angry with Andy and say that he never admits he is wrong. Andy will likely do the same with Melissa. And they will both be right!

Below, rewrite the dialogue between Andy and Melissa as it should be said.

Of course it is possible to use all the right words and not mean what you say. That's hypocrisy and has nothing to do with forgiving. When we practice forgiveness, our words flow from a humble heart that acknowledges how much we ourselves have been forgiven.

1. Is there a difference between an apology and asking for forgiveness?

Forgiving by Grace

It is one thing to gain clarity on what forgiveness is and what it isn't; it is quite another thing to actually practice it. As we worked through this lesson, we probably thought of people who have sinned against us. We may be troubled by the call to forgive them. We may also have thought of someone we have sinned against. We know we need to ask that person for forgiveness. Do either of these scenarios frighten you? It can be just as frightening to release someone from a debt as it is to admit to our own sin. By God's grace and by remembering the cost Jesus paid that we may be forgiven, it can be done!

The king in the parable who canceled such a tremendous debt is none other than Jesus. He emptied himself and bore our sin on the cross. His desire for reconciliation required absorbing a costly debt that we owed. How can we not do likewise? With God's grace, which he gives us abundantly, Heather will find the strength to forgive her abuser. Grace can forgive John. Andy and Melissa will practice forgiveness in their marriage day after day. Michael will be able to forgive his dad for his angry outburst. John will be able to confess his sin and ask Grace for forgiveness. Heather's abuser can find the strength to admit the evil he has done.

What about you? Will you focus on the debt that is owed you or will you focus on the debt that has been paid for you?

A Turkish officer raided and looted an Armenian home. He killed the aged parents and gave the daughters to the soldiers, keeping the eldest daughter for himself. Sometime later she escaped and trained as a nurse. As time passed, she found herself nursing in a ward of Turkish officers. One night, by the light of a lantern, she saw the face of this officer. He was so gravely ill that without exceptional nursing he would die. The days passed, and he recovered. One day, the doctor stood by the bed with her and said to him, "But for her devotion to you, you would be dead." He looked at her and said, "We have met before, haven't we?" "Yes," she said, "we have met before." "Why didn't you kill me?" he asked. She replied, "I am a follower of him who said 'Love your enemies.'"[1]

This true story, reveals a woman who knew what she had been forgiven. May we always remember, too, as we seek and grant true forgiveness.

Central Point

1. Forgiveness involves canceling a debt and absorbing the cost ourselves.
2. Forgiveness is both a past event and an ongoing process into the future.
3. We are called and given grace to always forgive even if reconciliation is not possible.

---

1. L. Gregory Jones, *Embodying Forgiveness: A Theological Analysis* (Grand Rapids: Eerdmans, 1995), 265–66.

Personal Application

1. I need to remember the debt Jesus absorbed on my behalf so that I might be forgiven.
2. I need to remember that God will treat me the same way I treat others.
3. I need to ask God for the grace to truly forgive and seek forgiveness.

Relational Application

1. I must fully forgive others by forfeiting my right to collect what is owed me by not bringing up the debt to the offender, to others, or to myself.
2. I must continue to forgive the offender each time I remember the sin against me.
3. I must seek forgiveness for my offenses by specifically naming my sin and asking for forgiveness.

Make It Real

1. What aspect of forgiveness do you struggle with most? Letting go of the hurt; absorbing the cost; not bringing up the sin again to the offender, to others, or to yourself; admitting your own sin; asking for forgiveness?

Make it a daily prayer that God will give you the grace to forgive or to seek forgiveness as you should.

2. Find a passage of Scripture that will help you remember what Christ has done for you (Matt. 18:21–35; Col. 2:13–15; 1 Pet. 1:1–9), and read it daily.

3. Pray and ask God to reveal anyone you need to forgive as he wants you to forgive. Forgive anyone whom you have not been willing to truly forgive. Pray and ask God to reveal to you anyone you need to ask forgiveness of. Go to those people, confess your sin specifically, and ask them to forgive you.

Preparing for Lesson 8: Look back at your list from lesson 2, all we have in Christ. Underline all the things on the list we will one day have but do not have yet. Add any other things that we have been promised but have not yet received.

Hope in the Middle

Review

Did you have opportunities this past week to forgive or seek for-giveness? Were there any passages of Scripture that have helped you remember what Christ has done for you so that you might more easily forgive others?

Central Point and Application

Central Point: My relationships will never be perfect; because of Christ, I cannot only make it through the difficulties, but I can be used by him as an instrument of his grace.

Personal Application: I need to remain in Christ so that I can bear fruit (patience, gentleness, humility) in my relationships.

Relational Application: I need to encourage others to remain in Christ.

THE BIG QUESTION
Why can relationships be so difficult,
and how can you get through it?

Opening Activity

What do you like most: being at the beginning, in the middle, or at the end of something? Why?

The problem with relationships is that they all take place right smack dab in the middle of something, and that something is the story of redemption—God's plan to turn everything in our lives into instruments of Christlike change and growth. You and I never get to be married to a fully sanctified spouse. We will never be in a relationship with a completely mature friend. We will never have self-parenting children. We will never live next to a neighbor utterly free of the need to grow and change. We will never be near people who always think, say, desire, or do the right things. And the reason for all of this is that our relationships are lived between the *already* and the *not yet*.

Share the list you created from lesson 7 of the promises we have not yet received. (See also Appendix D.)

Relationships in the Middle

Everyone who lives between the already and the not yet will experience four things. As we consider each of these areas, consider also the hope that we can have in response.

1. Our relationships will never work according to our plans.
Our relationships don't work according to our plans because they are part of *God's* plan. This often means God will take us where we have not planned to go in order to produce in us what we could not achieve on our own. He will lead us through the hardships of relationships so that our hearts will be revealed, our character strengthened, and we will become more and more like him.

a. Even though our relationships will never work according to our plans, what is the hope we have in Christ?

2. Our relationships will never live up to our expectations.
Our expectations often can follow closely from our dreams. And when it comes to relationships, we dream of unchallenged unity, unfettered romance, unobstructed communication, mutual cooperation, blanket acceptance and respect, shared decisions, intimate friendship, or an absence of conflict. Our expectations tend to forget that our relationships are being lived out in the middle of the already and the not yet. This side of eternity none of us gets to be with the person of our dreams, and none of us are ready to be the person of someone else's dream! At some point in every relationship, we are required to accept graciously who the other person is.

a. Even though our relationships will never live up to our expectations, what is the hope we have in Christ?

3. Our relationships will always grapple with some kind of difficulty.
Building relationships is like threading a needle while driving on a bumpy road! No relationship will be completely successful in avoiding the difficulties that are a normal part of life. Sometimes the difficulty will be the other person—pride, selfishness, greed, anger, bitterness, or impatience. Sometimes the difficulty will

reflect the reality of a fallen world—racism, persecution, injury, disease, war, mechanical failures, or an imperfect government, culture, and economy.

a. Even though our relationships will always grapple with some kind of difficulty, what is the hope we have in Christ?

4. Our relationships will always need to improve.
No matter how good even the best relationship is, room for improvement exists. Because we have not yet escaped our sin, our relationships will require difficult work and continued growth.

a. Even though our relationships will always need to improve, what is the hope we have in Christ?

The Hardship of Relationships in the Middle

The hardships of relationships are not only that they don't ever meet our expectations or follow our plans, or that they can just be difficult. The hardship includes the fact that God calls each of us to minister to the people God, in his wisdom, has placed in our lives in the midst of the difficulties. We are not called to only survive and bear with the weaknesses of others but to actually be used as instruments of grace in their lives. For this to occur requires humility to live with a sinner in a world of difficulty, gentleness to be part of what God is doing in someone's life and not get in the way, patience to deal with the sin and weaknesses of those around you, perseverance to not give in as change takes time, forgiveness, and forbearance to respond in love even when you are being provoked.

1. How do you feel about being called to be an instrument of change in another person's life?

Encouraging Others in the Middle

Life in the middle of the already and the not yet is difficult. Therefore, the skill and practice of encouragement is essential for a biblically healthy community. It is rare when encouragement is not timely, but even when we want to encourage someone, our encouragement can fall short. We tend to make two mistakes.

1. We think encouragement is primarily about making the other person feel better.

a. Can you think of some things we might say that focus on making the other person feel better?

b.   What can be wrong with this focus?

2.   We try to encourage the person by explaining what the prob-
     lem is and why it is happening.
We think that if the person understands what is going on, he
will be less anxious and more able to do things that are helpful
and constructive. There are occasions where this is true and when
it is important to gain insight and understanding, but explanation does not always comfort. Sometimes, the more accurate our
understanding the more discouraged we become—once we had a
superficial understanding, but now we know how deep the problem is and we are more overwhelmed than ever. Encouragement
must go deeper than providing understanding.

Real Encouragement. Real encouragement is more about sightedness than it is about explanation—not seeing with our physical eyes
but with the eyes of our heart. Spiritual sightedness is about seeing
unseen spiritual realities. The reason we get overwhelmed and discouraged in relationships is not because we don't understand what is going
on. We are discouraged because we don't see Christ. When the eyes of
our heart don't focus on Christ, we end up focusing on the immediate
difficulties. We see the husband who barely communicates. We see the
friend who has been consistently disloyal. We see the child who rebels
against every command. We see the boss who is unrelentingly critical. We see the relative who breaks every promise she ever makes. We
see the wife who is bitter and angry. We see neighbors who are more
concerned about boundaries than community. And the one thing that
can give us the hope and courage to go on becomes obstructed by the
looming problems. That one thing is Christ.
     As we live with one another in the middle of the already and
the not yet, we need more than elevated emotion and accurate

understanding. We need eyes to see this one amazing reality: that we are Christ's and he is ours. This is the encouragement we all need to hear and be refocused upon. We need to help others see three things so that they do not give up and lose hope in the middle of relational difficulties:

1. Christ's Presence: Your goal here is to help people develop a "Christ is with me" mentality.

Read Psalm 46:1–2.

a. What is the image of difficulty the psalmist creates?

b. What is the response the psalmist says we will have?

c. Why?

Even when cataclysmic things are happening, we can have peace because we know our powerful and glorious God is with us. Our hope does not rest on the shoulders of our own strength, wisdom, and character but on his. God is here and able to do what we could never do.

2. Christ's Promises: Though people may react negatively to hearing how Christ's promises speak to their situation—seeing them as spiritual trickery to make them feel good about something that is bothering them—those promises are the true identity of the believer. Christ's promises are not mystical, pie-in-the-sky unrealities but accurate assessments of the true resources we have as God's children.

3. Our Potential in Christ: When we struggle, we often begin to measure our potential. We assess ourselves to see whether we have what it takes to get through the difficulty. The problem is that most of us are poor personal accountants. When we add up the things that define our potential, we leave out the most important asset: Christ.

Read Galatians 2:20.

a. How does this verse help us to accurately view our potential?

Closing Activity

Small Group Sharing. Create groups of three to five people, and answer one of the following questions:

Think of a relationship you have (marriage relationship, parent-child relationship, small-group relationship, work relationship, etc.).

Has the relationship gone according to your plan? Is the relationship living up to your expectation? What difficulties is your relationship facing? What improvement could be made in the relationship? What from this lesson has encouraged you or given you hope?

Pray together and for one another.

Central Point

1. We are all in the middle of being redeemed and perfected.
2. My relationships will never be perfect.
3. God not only wants us to endure the process of redemption and perfection but to use us in the lives of others as a part of the process.

Personal Application

1. I can't expect my relationships to go according to my plan, expectations, or will.
2. I can have hope because of Christ's promises, presence, and potential.
3. I can be used by God in his work of redemption.

Relational Application

1. I need to be patient, humble, forbearing, gentle, and loving in my response to others because none of us is perfect (yet).
2. I can give hope to others by encouraging them to focus on Christ's promises, presence, and potential.

Make It Real

1. Decide whether you are willing to be an instrument of God's grace in the life of another. Pray for that person(s) daily. Pray that God will give you what you need to be an instrument of change in her life. Review lessons 4 and 5 as you seek to be God's instrument.

2. Decide whether you are willing to allow someone else to be God's instrument of grace in your life. What will you need to be or do to allow that person to help you grow in Christ?

3. Sit down with someone God has placed in your life and for whom you believe God has called you to be an instrument (your spouse, children, coworker, friend). Ask that person how you could best encourage him. What does he tend to forget or doubt about God's presence, promises, or potential?

Transforming Average Relationships into Great Relationships

Review

Have you identified someone to be God's instrument in your life? Did God use her this past week in your life? How? Have you been praying for those in whose lives you feel God wants to use you?

Central Point and Application

Central Point: Whoever wants to be great must become a servant.

Personal Application: What I say I believe and know about Jesus is only meaningful when I put it into action through service.

Relational Application: Because Jesus is my Master, I must serve others.

THE BIG QUESTION
What will it take to have a great relationship?

Opening Activity

What we know, what we believe, and what we say we believe do not automatically make successful relationships. What makes words powerful is the action that flows from them. What makes correct thinking about God powerful and meaningful is the life that emerges daily from that knowledge. We have talked a lot about thinking the correct way about our relationships, but that understanding is on display not in our words or our thinking but in how we actually treat others!

The Bible has many passages on what we should be doing for "one another" (often called the one-another passages). How many one-another commands can you name?

Read Mark 10:35–45.

1. What leads to the conflict among the disciples?

2. What truth does Jesus teach them?

The Actions of a Great Relationship

When we think about our relationships, how many of them ultimately revolve around making sure our concerns are heard and our self-defined "needs" are met? Start with those we love the most. I am married and have four children, and most of the time I am committed to thinking about how they can make my life more fulfilling. I know this is true because of how easily I get irritated when I have to give up personal comfort to serve them. This is with people I love; I haven't even begun to think about the difficult people. And I will not even bring up my enemies! Do you see this in yourself? This is the first step to becoming a servant and being great in our relationships. We must see how much of a servant we aren't before we can start to become one.

The disciples had to learn this, too, which means we are in good company. Twelve normal men had spent several years in Jesus' presence, and yet they were so thickheaded that they were vying for power and position. It was a lesson Jesus felt was important enough to stress even as he prepared for his death. John records for us in John 13 how Jesus intends for us to follow him. Through words and actions, Jesus gives his disciples instructions that will help them change the world.

Read John 13:1–17.

1.   From this passage what do we learn about what it means to be a leader and Christ's disciple?

Circumstances do not determine whether we serve. One of our most common excuses for not being more loving and helpful is our circumstances. When we are weighed down with difficulties, what is the first thing we want to do? We don't want to do anything! We want others to do things for us. We want to be served, not serve. Again, I only have to look as far back as yesterday for examples.

When my children press in on me the second they arrive from school, I am suddenly reminded of all my responsibilities. *Don't they understand I have a job with many things to think about? Why do they insist that I help them with their homework immediately? Don't they see that I have more important things to be concerned about than their assignments?* These are the thoughts that race through my mind. Soon I feel convicted about my impatience and try to rationalize it. *I would be more patient if I didn't have to worry about my bills and getting my work done. I would be a kinder, gentler father if they would be less aggressive and more obedient and respectful.*

In other words, if my circumstances were easier, I would be a better servant. If I could take care of my cares, I would be more caring. In fact, my children just got home from school as I was writing this, and I was tempted to get irritable—again!

2. What are Jesus' circumstances in John 13?

3. Yet what does Jesus do?

It would have been very tempting for Jesus to say, "Don't you guys know what is about to happen to me? Get a grip and comfort me!" Yet he says nothing about what is about to occur; he just serves, without self-pity.

This kind of serving is not normal—it is miraculous. When our circumstances are difficult, it feels like a miraculous act to serve someone else; but that is what Jesus did, and he calls his followers to do the same. We should never minimize the humble service of one person to another; it is a sign of God's grace at work in a person's life.

Someone's worthiness does not determine whether we serve. Jesus not only serves in the midst of his great crisis; he serves the very ones who don't deserve to be served. As Jesus' eyes scanned the room, I wonder what he was thinking. He sees Judas, who would soon betray him and hand him over to the Roman authorities. He sees Peter, who would soon deny that he was ever associated with Jesus. The other ten disciples would use the feet he is washing to run for cover when Jesus needs them most. And yet Jesus gets down on his knees and serves them all.

Think of all the areas of worthiness we consider when we are faced with serving someone. We consider whether they will properly appreciate what we have done, we consider past times when we were burned, we consider whether they will expect more, we consider whether they have done anything for us in the past or we consider how they have hurt us in the past, we consider their sin and their selfishness, or we consider how critical they might be. All of these considerations are weighing how worthy we feel the other person is. But Jesus calls us to serve and move into people's lives even when we risk being vulnerable, being unappreciated, being pushed and annoyed, unrecognized, even when it means serving the selfish and weak. Who tempts us to give up? Who in our lives has maxed out their compassion quotas? Jesus is calling us to serve those people. Think about the one or two people who have most significantly impacted your life for good. Weren't humility and servanthood a large part of their influence?

Our position does not determine whether we serve. Jesus is God; Creator and King of the universe (see John 13:1, 3), yet he chose to serve and to humble himself by washing his disciples' feet.

4. How is Jesus' example and definition of greatness very different from the examples and definitions the world gives us?

I can't think of any relationship where this notion is more frequently put to the test than with my children. The Bible clearly says that parents have authority over their children. Children are not to run the household; parents are. It would seem to follow that children are to serve the parents and not the other way around. Yet, at the same time, the Bible redeems authority from sinful patterns by humbling parents and calling them to use their authority for the benefit of the children. Where in your life do you have the privilege to serve people who are "under" you?

Doing the Miraculous

We stated earlier that serving in the midst of difficult circumstances, serving and overcoming our own self-centered nature, and serving those who are unworthy require a miracle. Fortunately, it is a miracle God desires to grant to each one of us.

The first part of the miracle happened when Jesus went to the cross on our behalf so that we might be washed and our sins forgiven so that the Holy Spirit could dwell within us. This is what Jesus meant when he said to Peter, "Unless I wash you, you have no part with me." Accepting God's grace in his gift of salvation is the first step to being able to show grace and to serve others.

The second part of the miracle is that by the Spirit we have the power to show grace and to serve others. This requires daily cleansing from God. It is what Jesus meant when he said to Peter, "A person who has had a bath needs only to wash his feet." Jesus means we are cleansed and justified by his death on the cross, but we still need daily cleansing and sanctification. We can't live only on past grace; we need present grace.

The moment we move out into the world we face trouble and temptation. We may become involved in conflict and persecution. There will be times when we want to quit and wonder if it is worth following Jesus. At these moments, we need the work of the Spirit to remind us of our own sin and remind us of the grace available to us. The service Jesus rendered for us in his life, death, and resurrection is not only for forgiveness of sins or for a future in heaven; it is also for the daily power to change in the present. We are not just promised life after death but also life before death!

Closing Activity

Serving Opportunities

What is it that tends to keep you from serving others? Circumstances—too busy, too focused on something else, too needy yourself? You look for examples of unworthiness as an excuse?

Central Point

1. Whoever wants to be great must become a servant.
2. Jesus is our model for perfect servanthood.

Personal Application

1. Serving others is never optional if I claim Jesus as my Lord.
2. I need to be reminded of my need for grace and forgiveness so I can offer grace and forgiveness to others.
3. I need to be mindful of how Christ served me so I can serve others.

Relational Application

1. I need to see myself as a servant in relation to others.
2. I can serve others by loving, accepting, honoring, carrying their burdens, and bearing with them.
3. I must look for opportunities to serve instead of looking for excuses not to serve.

Make It Real

1. What did you do this past week to serve your spouse, your children, your friend, your coworkers, or people in your church or small group? You say you love God, but do others know that based on your actions and your service?

2. Select three people: a loved one, a difficult person you usually avoid, and an enemy. Go through the one-another passages and pray, asking God to show how you could apply them to the three people.

Read the following descriptions as examples of what you can be considering.

-   Be devoted to one another in brotherly love (Rom. 12:10). How can I better treat this person with love and acceptance, like he is a part of my family? How can I rally around this person as if he were family?
-   Honor one another above yourselves (Rom. 12:10). I can honor someone by treating her seriously, by taking a backseat. How can I better honor the people I have in mind?
-   Accept one another just as Christ accepted you (Rom. 15:7). What is it about this person I don't accept? How do I exclude him? What nonessential, secondary convictions do I allow to get between another Christian and me?

- Carry each other's burdens (Gal. 6:2). What burden does the other person carry that I could bear alongside of her? (Some of the weight will fall on you. It may cut into your lifestyle and require sacrifice.) How could I ease that person's burden? Compassion; spending time with her; listening to her; using my gifts, abilities, or resources?
- Be completely humble and gentle; be patient, bearing with one another in love (Eph. 4:2). How can I be more patient with the person, especially when I am tempted to be irritated? What weaknesses and idiosyncrasies do I need to better tolerate?

3. Ask a loved one in your life, "If I could do one act of service this week for you, what could I do?" and then follow through on doing that act of service.

4. Read James 2:14–17 and 1 John 3:16–18. If you struggle in serving others, read these verses daily!

Time and Money

Review

What was an act of service you did this past week that you normally would not have done or did not really want to do but did it anyway because you remembered that you are called to serve others?

Central Point and Application

Central Point: God lavishes his resources and grace on us so that we may share them in the lives of others.

Personal Application: I need to spend quality time with God connecting with the source of grace to be able to give grace to others.

Relational Application: I need to give generously of my time and money to others.

THE BIG QUESTION
Will you chose to be a conduit or a cul-de-sac?

Opening Discussion

John Piper writes, "God is calling us to be conduits of his grace, not cul-de-sacs."

1. What does John Piper mean?

God loves people, and if we are to truly love God, we need to love people too. God treasures people and gave up his Son for our behalf: "He who did not spare his own Son, but gave him up for us all—how will he not also, along with him, graciously give us all things?" (Rom. 8:32). Our relationships should imitate this kind of sacrificial love.

One way to evaluate and discover what we treasure is to look at our schedules and our checkbooks. How we relate to time and money says a lot about our relationship to God and how we view other people. Ephesians 4:28 and 5:16 say important things about money and time. And interestingly, Paul slips these comments in amid teaching on relationships.

Money and People

Read Ephesians 4:25–32.

In this passage, Paul gives commands to the believer along with a reason or purpose for the command. So in verse 25, why should we speak truthfully? Because we are members of one body. In verse 27, what is the purpose behind not sinning in our anger? So we do not give the devil a foothold.

1. According to Paul in verse 28, what are the purposes for working?

What is your primary purpose for working and making money? Is it to provide for yourself and your family? To live securely? To be able to retire? To be able to be comfortable? Or can you truly say, "I primarily work so I can share what I make with others"? What do your investments say about what you think about yourself and others? Is there any indication that you are investing your money in the things God says are important? Or are you just building bigger and better barns that only serve your purposes?

Read 2 Corinthians 8:1–15.

In writing to the Corinthians, Paul makes two comparisons that provide clear examples of how to view our giving.

1. The Giving of the Macedonians

As we examine the giving of the Macedonians, compare their relationship to money to your own.

Their giving encouraged unity. The Macedonians were Gentiles, and they owed their spiritual lives to Jewish Christians. Their giving reflected this.

Read Romans 15:25–27. Here is a tangible expression of unity between Jewish and Gentile Christians. This is remarkable given the deep rift that existed between Jew and Gentile even in the early days of the church. Our experience of reconciling grace is expressed every time we pool our resources for the kingdom of God.

Their giving was a supernatural work of the Spirit. Second Corinthians 8:1 says that their giving was a sign of God's work in them. This kind of giving does not occur naturally. Their unified worship of the living God produced giving that was surprising and even shocking. Do you give as an expression of worship? Is your giving an overflow of the work God is doing in your heart?

Their giving was surprising. The Macedonians gave contrary to the way the world gives. They gave not out of abundance but rather despite their own need. In the midst of their poverty and persecution, they exhibited generosity and joy. This is an astounding contrast. The average person gives once he has enough to support his chosen lifestyle. If someone examined your giving, would she be surprised at how much you give?

Their giving was sacrificial. The Macedonians gave far more than they could afford (v. 3). Here we see the Macedonians making a difficult situation even more difficult for themselves by giving more. Most of us in this situation would limit our giving. Not the Macedonians! Not you?

Their giving was spontaneous. The Macedonians pleaded for the privilege of sharing and giving (v. 4). This was not a budgeted item but a sincere desire to give. Here is a poverty-stricken congregation pleading for the opportunity to give to their hurting Jewish brothers. Notice who is doing the begging here: It is not Paul! Paul is not coercing them with guilt. Do you beg to give away your resources? Are you working passionately to find ways to bless others?

Their giving was an act of submission. Were they submitting to Paul, the great apostle, or his visionary ministry? Neither, first they submitted to God and then to their brothers and sisters in Christ in Jerusalem. Their giving was caught up in their relationship to God and their solidarity with their spiritual family. Are you willing to submit your finances to God's will and provision?

2. The Giving of Jesus

Paul uses the Macedonians as an example of generosity as well as Jesus himself who "though he was rich, yet for your sakes he became poor, so that you through his poverty might become rich" (v. 9). The motivation to give generously should be more than a moral code and more than the guideline of a tithe; it should flow from a gratitude to Jesus who gave all he had for us. Do you remember your past spiritual poverty and the riches you have been given?

God intends for us to be a conduit of his grace, which includes his grace of material blessing. Examine your relationship to money. What does it tell you about your relationship to God? What does it reveal about what you think is most important?

Time and People

Apart from sleeping, how do we spend most of our time? Like money, our use of time is a window into our souls. It reveals to what degree we are being transformed by the grace of Christ and how much of a conduit we are of that grace.

Read Ephesians 5:15–21.

Like his comments about money in Ephesians 4:28, Paul connects his comments about time to our relationships with other Christians and the world.

1. What do you think Paul means when he writes, "making the most of every opportunity because the days are evil"?

The King James translates the phrase "making the most of every opportunity" as "redeeming the time." The Greek word for time used here is not *chronos*, which refers to the passing of time in hours, months, and years. Instead, *kairos* is used, which the Bible uses to refer to the time between Jesus' first and second comings. This is a time of unique opportunity for us to display the grace of Christ to others. One day this season will come to an end when Christ returns in power and glory. Thus a more awkward but appropriate rendering of this verse would be, "As you go about your life in this 'in-between time' use it to its fullest to display the grace of Christ to others." In light of this knowledge, how do we understand what this verse is asking of us?

- It is not calling for frenetic activity. This passage is not encouraging activity that overloads our schedules with church events and obligations. Nor does it ask us to turn normal relational moments into abnormal witnessing encounters. In fact, this kind of behavior may hinder us from living wisely. Using our time wisely may include formal ministry opportunities such as a missions trip, teaching a Sunday school class, or working in the nursery, but the call here is not so much about specific activities as it is about a lifestyle committed to God's purposes, encompassing all the details of daily life.

- It means that we see our lives in light of our various callings. This passage is saying, "Make the most of every area in which God has placed you." Are you single, married, retired, parent, child, friend, employer, employee, student, grandparent? These are all callings and seasons of life, and we are to see them as opportunities to display the grace of Christ. Our tendency is to live with a get-through-this-season mentality. We think, *If I can just get through this busy season of life, then I will be okay. If I can just get through the diaper phase, . . .* (or the elementary years or the teenage years). Or, *Once I get married, . . .* Or, *Once I have children . . . .* If we are not careful, we will wish our lives away and miss many opportunities to love and serve others. God wants to use the daily struggles of life as critical moments of redemptive opportunity rather than hindrances or distractions.

- It means that we are to seize the little moments of life. Did you know that 95 percent of our life is lived in the mundane? For example, suppose a husband and wife are upset with each other. Will they turn toward each other, or will they remain angry? This is a mammoth redemptive moment—huge! Consider how many of these moments we miss every day. Imagine if this couple misses thousands of these over the course of their marriage. Where will their marriage be in twenty years? Imagine if, instead, they took advantage of these times. Can you see the difference this would make?

- We must see the context in which these things take place. Paul says, "Because the days are evil." We live in war zones. We get out of bed every morning, and there are battles raging for our souls, our lives, our friendships, and our marriages. We can't afford to waste these moments. The war is won in the little skirmishes that take place throughout our lives. "Wake up!" Paul says. "You are at war."

Money, Time, and People

God lavishes his resources on us so that we might participate and use those resources in his kingdom work. Do other people share in God's blessings to you, or do you hoard them all for yourself? We are called to love God and to use his blessings to love others. But sadly, we often use other people to get the things we love.

When I got married, I did what every other groom does. I repeated vows to my wife that said I would love her sacrificially all the days of my life. Who was I kidding? I look back and see how little I understood what I promised. What I was really thinking to a large degree was, *This is great! I love me, and now you are going to love me!* My love was quite shallow. It only took a few days of marriage to figure that out! God had plans to use my wife and children to show me just how shallow my love was and to help it deepen as I saw how much I needed to grow. Seeing this caused me to depend on God and his grace all the more.

Not a day passes that I don't struggle with the way I use my time and money with my family. And these are people I say I love! I struggle to hold my time loosely when I don't want to be disturbed. I find myself flinching when one of my children asks me for a few dollars to go out with friends. These daily reminders reveal a heart still in need of a major overhaul. The only thing capable of penetrating the hardness of my heart is the gracious redemption that Father, Son, and Spirit have accomplished on my behalf. If my heart is going to be changed, it has to remain immersed in his grace.

Think about a steak. If you want it to be tender and flavorful, you will put it in a marinade for a while before you place it on the grill. If we are going to love others with our time and money, something similar needs to happen with our hearts. Our hearts are hard and full of gristle; the way to soften them is to let them soak in God's redemptive grace in Christ. This is the only thing powerful enough to loosen our grip on money and time and produce real change. The gospel reminds us that everything we have is from God.

Closing Activity

Spend time writing a note of encouragement to someone. It could be a pastor, elder, deacon, teacher, family member, neighbor, coworker, and so on. Write as many as possible in the time provided. A note of encouragement can greatly spur others onto love and bless them. Consider choosing one or two of the people you wrote to and include a monetary gift or gift card. Imagine the influence you could have by giving your boss a letter of encouragement and a gift card to a local restaurant. Or think about how encouraged an elder might feel by your note and gift. How often do they have someone thank them for the work they do in the church? Or when is the last time you said something positive or encouraging to your spouse or child and gave them an unexpected gift?

Central Point

1. My time and money are given to me by God's grace.
2. God lavishes his resources and grace on me so that I may share them in the lives of others.

Personal Application

1. God expects me to use what he has given me in the lives of others, not to hold back for any reason.
2. I need to spend quality time with God connecting with the source of grace to be able to give grace to others.
3. My growth in grace requires I give grace to others through the use of my time and money.

Relational Application

1. I need to give generously of my time and money to others.
2. I need to see others as God does—as a treasure worth sacrificing for and investing in.

Make It Real

1. Being a conduit of God's grace will require commitment and submission to God. Make a list of commitments you could make as a

result of this lesson. For example: Commit to spending time/more time with God each morning; commit to increasing your tithe; commit to giving beyond what you feel you could give; commit to spending a set amount of time with your spouse/children each day; commit to adding a missionary or other charity to your yearly spending; and so on.

Pray, and then if you are married, compare your list with your spouse's list. As a couple, select the ones you really feel God is calling you to commit to.

2. Go through your clothes, selecting only what you really need, and give away the rest.

3. Choose four people or couples you would like to reach out to. Invite them to dinner—one each week of a month.

Preparing for lesson 11: Review the principles in lesson 8, especially the principles on encouraging others.

Review Lessons 1–10: Application Case Study

Review

We have discussed three practical ways to love others we are in relationship with: serving, giving of our money, and giving of our time. Have you made any improvement in one of these three areas over the past weeks? What has made it more difficult, or what has made it easier?

Explanation Is Not Enough

When we are in the midst of trying circumstances, our tendency is to search for an explanation that does three things:

1. Helps us understand what is going on: We want to understand our struggle. We want to know why the other person is acting as he is. We want to know why he feels the way he does. How did the other person change into someone so unpleasant? These are very good questions.

2. Points us to where we should be going: when things are difficult, a time comes when we give up on grander purposes and settle

for survival. We stop asking, "What can be?" and ask instead, "Will I make it?" We want goals that will give us purpose and motivation and direction. These, too, are good desires.

3. Tells us how to get there: after seeing what is going on and where we need to be, we want practical skills and an action plan to get there. These good things should also not be minimized.

However, despite these positive elements, explanations alone will only increase our despair over time. Some initial encouragement and hope may exist, but it will not last because explanations alone can convince us that the problems are deeper than we thought, the goals farther away, and our practical skills inadequate for the difficulty. We don't need something less than explanation; we need something more.

Activity 1

Often people who are experiencing problems in relationships need encouragement first, not solutions and not fault finding. They need someone who will listen intently with empathy and encouragement, not make them feel condemned or minimize the problem. Read the following case study and then, using the principles in lesson 8, consider what you would say to Brian and Kara to encourage them.

Brian and Kara had been married for eight years. They were facing a mountain of problems. Both had grown up in privileged families and been given all that life had to offer. Both sets of parents had high expectations for their futures and had provided everything they believed essential for success. Brian, Kara, and their siblings had been expected to take advantage of all these opportunities and use them to attain excellence.

Brian and Kara responded to their upbringings quite differently. Born much later than his siblings, Brian always lived in their shadows. His brother was a prominent surgeon, and his sister was a high-powered lawyer in a top firm. Brian felt as though all eyes were on him, wondering how he would match their achievements. In his third year of college, the cracks began to show. After several semesters of near-failing grades in his pre-law classes, he decided to study philosophy. This was deeply disappointing to his parents, and they were quite vocal about it. They also orchestrated calls of "concern" from his brother and sister to reinforce the message. Brian's struggle with depression started at that time.

Kara, on the other hand, was the oldest of four children. She was the recipient of her parents' encouragement and never suffered the comparisons that Brian did. Those years of encouragement gave her the confidence to believe she could do almost anything. She finished her undergraduate degree with honors and went on to graduate from law school at the top of her class.

When Brian and Kara met, it seemed like the perfect match. Kara was drawn to Brian's pensive, sensitive personality. He was her retreat from the pressures of performance. Brian was drawn to Kara because she was like his family in many ways; he knew his parents would approve. Their common childhood experiences made it easy for them to talk to each other. It was so easy, in fact, that it kept them from seeing that they were two very different people.

Brian's sensitivity and Kara's achievements at first functioned as the bond in their relationship, but they later became the fault line at the center of their problems. Kara did not realize until after they were married that Brian had abandoned the achievement dream she cherished. She didn't know that their relationship would challenge everything that was important to her professionally, materially, socially, and personally. Brian didn't realize that Kara would expect the same things of him as his parents did. As their marriage went on, an unhealthy dynamic developed. Brian slid deeper into depression as he realized that he was not living up to Kara's expectations. Kara responded to Brian's apathy and depression by incessantly pushing and prodding him to accomplish something and by complaining when he failed to complete even menial jobs around the house. However, the more Kara tried to control Brian, the more he withdrew. It was a vicious spiral that was taking them both down.

The fallout was evident on many levels. Brian was starting his sixth job as a part-time philosophy professor at the local community college. Kara had created an Internet business that allowed her to stay home with their two children. The income from these two jobs didn't even come close to the lavish lifestyles they had once known. Their apartment embarrassed them; they didn't invite their families over because it only reminded them of their failure. Because Brian tended to avoid conflict and Kara tended to confront, their conversations got ugly fast, even on small matters. They couldn't agree on parenting decisions, so their relationships with their children suffered. Their friendships at their local church suffered too. Though they tried to maintain a positive appearance, the tension between them made it increasingly awkward for others to be around them. Brian has faded deeper into depression, and Kara is at the end of her rope.

1. Why is it important to first encourage Brian and Kara as opposed to trying to help solve the problems?

2. Men: What could you say to Brian to encourage him?

3. Women: What could you say to Kara to encourage her?

4. What could you say to show them God's present grace in their lives—that God has not abandoned them but is working on their behalf?

5. What promises from God could you share with them as encouragement?

6. What could you say to them as a reminder that in Christ healing and change are possible?

Activity 2

Take on the role of Brian or Kara. What change in your perspective will help you move toward God's grace? How will you need to view the conflict and difficulties? How will Kara need to view Brian and vice versa? How will their worship of God help change their perspective for change to begin? How will they need to view their identity for change to occur? What is the desire in their hearts that has lead to conflict? How might forgiveness play a crucial role, and what should that forgiveness look like? What ways of serving will help bring about change and provide mutual support?

Review

For further review and reinforcement, read Appendix E.

Moving Out

Review

What area(s) of your relationships have improved because of the ideas from this study that you have tried to put into practice?

Central Point and Application

Central Point: Our relationships are intended to attract others to the King.

Personal Application: I need to work and improve my relationships so I can be a testimony of God's grace to others.

Relational Application: I need to take opportunities God provides to be an example of his grace to others.

THE BIG QUESTION
Will you allow God to use your relationships to help others in theirs?

Opening Activity

Pray. Give thanks and praise God for his grace that you have seen since beginning this study. Give God thanks for the people he has in your life. Ask God for continued grace to grow and mature in your relationships. Ask God to reveal to you anything that you should seek forgiveness for.

The Kingdom of God

Once, having been asked by the Pharisees when the kingdom of God would come, Jesus replies, "The kingdom of God does not come with your careful observation, nor will people say, 'Here it is,' or 'There it is,' because the kingdom of God is within you" (Luke 17:20–21).

In a conversation with the Pharisees, Jesus confronts their fundamental misunderstanding of the kingdom of God. They imagine a system of political rule in which they would be the ruling class. Jesus informs them that his kingdom is not a system but the tangible display of the King's presence.

Because the Pharisees are looking for an earthly, political kingdom, they are looking to the future for its arrival. They are confused about what the visible display of the kingdom would be like. Many people conclude from this passage that the kingdom is not visible, but that it resides in the hearts of people. The NIV reinforces this view by translating the last phrase to read "the kingdom of God is within you." But Jesus is saying, "The kingdom of God is in your midst," pointing to an internal *and* external reality.

Jesus is telling the Pharisees that the kingdom is right there for them to see, but they do not see it. He is saying that, because the King is here, there are visible signs of his rule. What are these signs that go against what the Pharisees expect?

Jesus is pointing to an internal reality of grace that expresses itself in observable changes in individuals and their relationships. It leaves a trail of humility, compassion, sacrifice, joy, and patience, along with many other qualities. The impact of this revolution will extend to institutions and systems, but this is not where it begins. It begins in the hearts of people and has ripple effects that spread to the farthest reaches of sin. Jesus is saying that the Pharisees are looking at the very King of the kingdom while wondering when the promised kingdom is going to come!

If you are experiencing humility, forgiveness, compassion, patience, or godly conflict, you are experiencing that work of the King as he builds his kingdom. This means that your relationships are a place where the kingdom has come, and they are intended to attract others to the King!

In addition, whenever we speak of change in our lives and relationships, we are not drawing attention to our wisdom, relational savvy, or personal giftedness; we are calling attention to Jesus, our King. The kingdom of God is not only for private enjoyment but also for public display. People who come into our midst will see the work of the kingdom, but they won't necessarily see the King. It is our responsibility and privilege to point them to him.

The Visible Kingdom: Salt and Light

Read Matthew 5:13–16.

Salt

1. If we consider salt as a preserving element, how are we to be salt in the world?

2. If we consider salt as a flavoring, how are we to be salt in the world?

What ministry opportunities exist for you with the people God has put in your path?

Is a family struggling in your neighborhood? Is a single parent at your child's school? Is someone in your church lonely and discouraged? Does a teenager need to see how a family functions? Are there relationships you can pursue through your children's extracurricular activities? Where are the needs for service, mercy, and help in your community? Has God put an elderly person in your life who needs companionship? Where are the poor in your community? How can you be a part of their lives?

With some of these ways God may be moving you outward. You are not necessarily called to do all these things because of other callings and responsibilities you may already have, but God has undoubtedly given you opportunities to be salt. If you have children, you are called to care for them, but one way to care for them is to include them in some ministry opportunities God has given you.

Light

1. If, as salt, our character and presence in the world helps keep away decay, what aspect of light do we represent for the world?

2. If salt involves stepping out into the world, what does being light involve?

3. What should people see in our relationships?

What opportunities do you have to invite others into the light so they can see the kingdom? Does your child have a friend who may benefit from time in your house? Could you invite a coworker for dinner and a movie with your friends? Do you know an elderly person who would enjoy the love of a family during the holidays? Is there someone who is burdened or in crisis and in need of a retreat? Is there another family who would enjoy time with your family? Do you know an older couple who could mentor a younger couple? If you are single, what family with young children could benefit from your help? How might this bless you as well?

Being Transparent

One thing is certain: in order to be salt and light, we must be confident in the God who entered a sinful world to redeem it. Though we are to be wise, we are not to fear the world in which God has placed us. Yes, things will get messy. But if we are humbled by the messiness of sin in our own lives, yet confident in God's grace to change us, we will not be afraid to get close to other sinners who need the same grace. God will use the messiness we encounter in others to spur our own growth in the gospel.

In Ephesians 5:11, Paul calls us to "expose" the "deeds of darkness." The word Paul uses for "exposing" the darkness does not mean "point the finger and judge." It means that we persuade people that the gospel is true because our lives are a compelling testimony to the God who has come for sinners.

Being a Worshipper

This call we have considered in this lesson is also a call to worship, not only a call to ministry and transparency. That might sound strange, but whenever we serve others, we are not only serving them; we are serving the King—and that is worship. Love for Christ will always extend itself to others. Thankfulness to Christ will always result in sharing our blessings with others. Enjoying the benefits of Christ's forgiveness will always express itself in forgiveness to others. Gratitude for God's loving pursuit will always lead us to pursue others—even when they don't want to be pursued. Thankfulness for Christ's willingness to enter our messy world will make us willing to enter someone else's. Worship recognizes that our good relationships do not belong to us but to Christ. Therefore, we cannot hoard them; we are compelled to share them with others. Jesus said, "The King will reply, 'I tell you the truth, whatever you did for one of the least of these brothers of mine, you did for me'" (Matt. 25:40).

Life at the Intersection

Ben and Erin met when they were teenagers. Their friendship quickly became romantic because they felt as if they had stumbled on a kind of love they never received at home. They found refuge in each other. Within a few months Erin was pregnant, and they faced the first of many difficult decisions. The embarrassment of the pregnancy led them to get married secretly, but they had little understanding of how to live together, and they didn't have a clue about how to love each other.

Ben was a boy in a man's body. He seemed more interested in the latest video game than the responsibilities of a husband and a father.

He was a latchkey kid who had never been accountable to others. Erin's parents were divorced. They tried to make up for it by giving her lots of gifts and indulging her every whim. She had been pampered in all the wrong ways and expected this kind of treatment as an expression of love. Ben did not have the desire or the resources to meet those expectations. Although he had made significant efforts to win her affection while they were dating, this changed as soon as they were married.

Erin's disappointment and Ben's feelings of failure, coupled with their inability to resolve conflict, turned the marriage into a war zone. Erin complained that Ben did not really love her; Ben complained that Erin was too demanding. They alternated between heated argument and cool withdrawal. In either case, they always pointed the finger at the other.

One evening their conflict spilled out into the stairwell of their apartment complex. Another couple overheard the argument and decided to ask if they could help. As a result of this simple act of kindness, Erin began to meet with the wife and Ben started a friendship with the husband. They also spent time together as couples.

These new friends were part of a local church that excelled in welcoming struggling people and discipling them in grace. Ben and Erin immediately found other couples who honestly shared about their struggles, which turned out to be surprisingly similar to their own. As people shared, what caught Ben and Erin's attention was the honesty that was tied to a strong hope for change. Significant personal changes began to take place in Ben and Erin as they came to trust in Christ. This simple yet powerful experience of the benefits of the gospel began to transform their marriage. They still had plenty of difficulty, but they began to deal with it differently. They were also surrounded by believers who were committed to reach out to them and persevere with them through the messy process of change now underway.

The Real Story

The story about Ben and Erin is really a story about an unnamed couple and the quietly revolutionary community of faith to which they belong. The weapons of their warfare were humility, honesty, hope, grace, and courage. They moved toward Ben and Erin and invited them into their own private world.

What this couple did can be summarized by one word from the Bible: kingdom. The revolution of the kingdom of God is not noisy and explosive. It's a quiet revolution carried out by humble servants who often go unnoticed. Just consider the King of this radical new kingdom. How did Jesus enter human history? He came as a baby born into poverty amidst an oppressed people. He preached a message of hope that advanced through the quiet but powerful display of God's love through his suffering, death, and resurrection. Wherever this King is present, these same surprising virtues will be present. These were the qualities that won Ben's and Erin's hearts.

What was it that drew Ben and Erin to this anonymous couple? Ben and Erin were fearful, hopeless, and desperate, but this anonymous couple was compelling. Their lives spoke of the power, hope, and reality of King Jesus. Ben and Erin felt as if they could trust them with their troubles. They, in turn, were willing to have their lives disrupted by needy people such as Ben and Erin. Whenever God's grace changes our hearts and lives, we are experiencing the kingdom coming to earth as it already is in heaven. And when we experience this kingdom power in our lives, we want others to experience it too.

Closing Activity

Celebrating What God Has Done

Central Point

1. Our relationships are intended to attract others to the King.
2. Whenever God's grace changes our heart and lives, we are experiencing God's kingdom coming to earth.

Personal Application

1. I need to work and improve my relationships so I can be a testimony of God's grace to others.
2. I need to be willing for others to see my own weaknesses and need for God's grace.

Relational Application

1. I need to take opportunities God provides to be an example of his grace to others.
2. I need to be part of other people's lives.

Make It Real

1. Make a list of people God has placed in your life to whom you feel convicted to be salt and light. Pray for these people.

2. Call and speak to one of these people, and invite him or her to join you in something you already have planned this week.

3. Look back at the questions under "Salt" and "Light." Whose life does God want you to have a larger role in?

Ephesians 1–3

Things We Have Received

- Every spiritual blessing in Christ (1:3)
- Adoption as sons (1:5)
- Grace (1:6–7; 2:7–8)
- Redemption (1:7)
- Forgiveness of sins (1:7)
- Knowledge of his will (1:9)
- The Holy Spirit (1:13)
- Citizenship (2:19)

Things We Are Called To

- Be holy and blameless (1:4)
- The praise of his glory (1:12, 14)
- Hope in his power (1:18)
- Be seated with Christ in the heavenly realms (2:6)
- Do good works (2:10)
- Be members of his household (2:19–22)

Ambassadors— Game Simulation

Divide the group based on the approximate number of people participating.

> 10 (A=5; B=4; C=1)
> 15 (A=7; B=6; C=2)
> 25 (A=13; B= 8; C=4)

The leader sends group C out of the room so that he can explain the roles of groups A and B.

"Group A, I want you to stand/sit here on this side of the room. Group C will be giving you items from me. Accept them without saying anything; in fact, you may not speak once the exercise begins. Any questions?

"Group B, I need you to divide into two lines making an aisle leading to group A from the opposite side of the room. [For example: if the aisle consists of six people, three people are on each side of the aisle with room for someone to walk between them.] I'm going to give each person in Group C different items to give to the people in Group A. For instance, I will tell [person from Group C] to give this penny to Jack and this water bottle to Jenny. When Group C begins walking between you toward Group A, I want you to try and get them to forget. So you might say to them, 'Give the penny to Jenny.' Once the group begins handing out the items, I want you to get them to go faster. This could include phrases such as, 'Come on, you want to be the fastest!'; 'Don't think, just do it!'; 'Hurry up so other people can have a turn!'"

The leader has Group C return and stand with him on the opposite side of Group A. The leader has enough items for each person in Group C to give at least one item to each person in Group A.

Therefore, if there are fifteen people total (see above), the leader will need at least fourteen items. The leader explains to the people of Group C which items he wants them to give to each of the people in Group A. [The leader should have it written down in advance.] For instance, "Give the ball to Tiffany"; "Give this apple to Ben," and so on. If the people in Group C do not know everyone in Group A, the leader should have the people in Group A raise their hands as he says their names.

Debriefing

Ask the people of Group C what made this task difficult.
Possible Responses:

- "It was difficult to remember which item to give to whom." Ask: What could have made it easier to remember? Possible responses: If it were written down. Parallel: We do have instructions written down in God's Word, but if we don't refer to it often, we too easily forget. We forget that God has instructed us to be patient, gentle, humble, and so forth.
- "It was more difficult because of the people distracting me." Ask: Is there anything in our lives that can distract us from fulfilling God's commands? Possible responses: Yes, our own sin nature, the deceitfulness of sin, the attractiveness of the world, other people telling us what to do, business, and so on.
- "It would have been easier if the people in Group A had talked to me and told me their names."

Ask the people of Group C whether they began trying to go faster when the group started telling them to go faster. Parallel: That is a lot like us when we follow agendas other than God's. For example, we are influenced by the world telling us to please ourselves, to make ourselves important, and to collect material wealth and possessions.

Ask the whole group, "Who did Group C represent?" Answer: It represented the leader who gave them the items to distribute. "How is that like us?" Answer: We represent Christ. (This is why the game is called Ambassadors.)

Lesson 6 Closing Activity

Understand that conflict is one way God works in our lives. Both Troy and Angela need to accept that the conflict happened and believe that it is okay because God wants to use it in both of their lives. The conflict itself is in the past; the future is now an opportunity to grow.

Identify what drives ungodly conflict in your life. Both Troy and Angela have sinned in the situation. Angela's tone in addressing Troy is disrespectful and unloving, as is Troy's tone to Angela. Troy's sinful desire was comfort or pleasure as he justified sitting on the couch. Angela's sinful heart's desire was possibly acceptance—perhaps she was fearful of being judged by Troy's parents—or control as she sought to make sure everything was in its proper place.

Recognize your default strategy in conflict. Troy and Angela also need to consider what they did to fuel the conflict. Troy was unwilling to be wrong; instead of communicating what he was thinking in love, he responded defensively and with sarcasm. He is placing being right above his wife. Angela was quick to assume and make accusations instead of sincerely giving Troy a chance to explain himself. She left the conflict as a way of staying in control and punishing Troy.

Engage in specific and intelligent spiritual warfare. Both Troy and Angela need to believe the true battle is taking place in their hearts and they need God's grace. Both should stop and pray and seek God's grace and truth.

Consider the other person. Both Troy and Angela ended the conflict by focusing on themselves. They need to consider what the other person needs.

Make a plan to approach the person.

- Own whatever personal sin you have brought to the situation. When Troy and Angela come together, the best chance for successful conflict resolution will be related to how willing they are to admit to their own sin. If each begins the process by proving he or she is right and the other wrong, they are only creating more conflict. Both Troy and Angela have identified the sin of their hearts and how they handled the issue and need to begin by confessing to the other.

- Agree together that you want God's will. This can take the focus off of yourself and remind you that God wants to use the conflict for your growth. It also gives you both the same focus as you move forward.
- Name the problem. This is the opportunity to explain your side of the conflict, but it should still focus on your own heart. For instance, Angela can begin by saying, "I got upset because I was fearful of being judged by your parents, and I didn't give you a chance to explain why you didn't clear the dishes as you said you would. What were you thinking?" Now Troy needs to be honest and explain what he was thinking. It could be a repetition of his initial confession, that he was seeking comfort over serving, or he may say that when he agreed to do it, he didn't mean immediately.
- Explore possible solutions. If Troy really was planning to do it later, then Troy and Angela need to come up with a solution so that miscommunication or unspoken expectations do not occur the next time.

Living Between the Already and the Not Yet

Already

- Jesus has provided salvation.
- The power of sin is broken.
- We are a new creation.
- We have come through difficulty.
- God has established his kingdom in our hearts.

Not Yet

- God's full saving work is not complete in us.
- Presence of sin has not been removed.
- We are not all that we will be in Christ.
- We still have trials to go through.
- God's kingdom is not fully come.

One-Another Passages

The "One Another" Passages

- Love one another: John 13:34–35; 15:12, 17;
  Romans 12:10; 13:8; 14:13; 1 Thessalonians 3:12; 4:9;
  2 Thessalonians 1:3; 1 Peter 1:22; 1 John 3:11, 23;
  4:7, 11–12; 2 John 1:5
- Serve one another: Galatians 5:13; Philippians 2:3;
  1 Peter 4:9; 5:5
- Accept one another: Romans 15:7, 14
- Strengthen one another: Romans 14:19
- Help one another: Hebrews 3:13; 10:24
- Encourage one another: Romans 14:19; 15:14; Colossians 3:16;
  1 Thessalonians 5:11; Hebrews 3:13; 10:24–25
- Care for one another: Galatians 6:2
- Forgive one another: Ephesians 4:32; Colossians 3:13
- Submit to one another: Ephesians 5:21; 1 Peter 5:5
- Commit to one another: 1 John 3:16
- Build trust with one another: 1 John 1:7
- Be devoted to one another: Romans 12:10
- Be patient with one another: Ephesians 4:2; Colossians 3:13
- Be interested in one another: Philippians 2:4
- Be accountable to one another: Ephesians 5:21
- Confess to one another: James 5:16
- Live in harmony with one another: Romans 12:16
- Do not be conceited toward one another: Romans 13:8
- Do not pass judgment on one another: Romans 14:13; 15:7
- Do not slander one another: James 4:11
- Instruct one another: Romans 15:14

- Greet one another: Romans 16:16; 1 Corinthians 16:20; 2 Corinthians 13:12
- Admonish one another: Colossians 3:16
- Spur one another on toward love and good deeds: Hebrews 10:24
- Meet with one another: Hebrews 10:25
- Agree with one another: 1 Corinthians 16:20
- Be concerned for one another: Hebrews 10:24
- Be humble to one another in love: Ephesians 4:2
- Be compassionate to one another: Ephesians 4:32
- Do not be consumed by one another: Galatians 5:14–15
- Do not anger one another: Galatians 5:26
- Do not lie to one another: Colossians 3:9
- Do not grumble to one another: James 5:9
- Give preference to one another: Romans 12:10
- Be at peace with one another: Romans 12:18
- Sing to one another: Ephesians 5:19
- Be of the same mind as one another: Romans 12:16; 15:5
- Comfort one another: 1 Thessalonians 4:18; 5:11
- Be kind to one another: Ephesians 4:32
- Live in peace with one another: 1 Thessalonians 5:13
- Carry one another's burdens: Galatians 6:2[1]

1. © 2000 Into Thy Word Ministries www.intothyword.org

Review Lessons 1–10: Application Case Study

Seeing the Unseen: Reflections on Kara and Brian

Kara's understanding of her situation is distorted by what she does not see. Let's say that someone has a ten-thousand-dollar debt but does not know that an inheritance of one hundred thousand dollars is coming. Won't that affect the way the person looks at the debt? Kara and Brian see their set of ten-thousand-dollar problems, but they do not see the billion-dollar provision God has made available to them. What they lack is not explanation but imagination.

Imagination is not the ability to dream up things that aren't real; it is the ability to see what is real but often unseen. Whenever parents help their child with homework, they imagine the child's future high school and college years. When a couple sits down to discuss finances, they anticipate their future retirement. Parents saving for a special vacation encourage their children to imagine what it will be like; it takes the sting out of the sacrifices needed to afford it. When the children complain, the parents remind them of the fun times ahead. The children learn to live with hardships because they are learning to see the unseen.

Imagination gives us a better sense of two unseen realities: our identities—the unseen realities of who God says we are—and God's resources—the unseen realities of his presence and provision with and for us.

Identity: Who Am I?

Imagine standing in an art gallery where the walls are covered with beautiful paintings. The only problem is that the lights are out and you can't see them! Imagine that wonderful music is playing but your ears are plugged with cotton. Imagine that you are eating an exquisite meal, but a head cold causes the flavors to run over your tongue unnoticed. This is what is true of Kara spiritually. She cannot see and experience the things that are true because she lacks spiritual sight, hearing, and taste. Her perspective is dominated by what is wrong in her life and relationships. They are the realities she lives by. Imagination, or faith, does not mean that Kara should deny her present circumstances; it does mean, however, that she should see them in the context of the whole picture, which includes who she is in Christ.

We often miss the unseen things that are true of us as God's children. But the Bible says that two fundamental things characterize those who are in Christ. First, a radical change has taken place in the core of our being. The Bible says that hearts of flesh have replaced our hearts of stone. Ezekiel 36:26 says, "I will give you a new heart and put a new spirit in you; I will remove from you your heart of stone and give you a heart of flesh." Paul is referring to the same thing when he says we are a new creation in Christ (2 Cor. 5:17). This wonderful reality does not mean that we have become perfect, but that our hearts are malleable, sensitive, and alive to God.

For Kara and Brian, this amazing truth means that they are *not* stuck, even though they are obviously struggling in their marriage. But they need imagination (that is, faith) to see their true potential for change. We often get stuck when repeatedly confronted with problems, failure, weakness, disappointment, and sin. Our track record tends to convince us that change is impossible. Imagination does not deny the track record but places it in the context of who we are in Christ. It reminds us that God's Spirit is at work in us, and that we are participants "in the divine nature" (2 Pet. 1:4). Thus God has gifted Brian and Kara with the potential for change.

Second, the Bible also stirs our imagination by explaining our connection to God as his children. Our new standing is legal, but it is also personal and practical. Marriage and adoption both involve legal unions but ones that are intended to create relationships that are far more than legal contracts. Imagine a married couple who only related at a legal level without love. Their marriage would be no different than a business partnership. What if adoptive parents only related to their new child in terms of their legal obligations to feed, clothe, and educate him? The words "I love you" would never be uttered. This would be horrific because the new legal status is intended to be the context in which a deeper, fuller relationship flourishes. Marital and parent-child relationships are not less than legal; they are so much more!

In the same way, our reconciliation with God gives us a relationship with him that should alter the way we respond to everything. God is now my Father, and I am his child. He looks on me with favor. I am the object of his attention and affection. I have access to his care. He blesses me with his resources. He offers ongoing forgiveness and cleansing as I struggle with sin. He promises never to leave or forsake me. He makes a commitment to finish the work of change he has begun in me.

Brian and Kara attend a good church where their new legal standing with God has been taught, but their personal understanding has remained theoretical. They have never learned how to connect it to their everyday experience so, while it sounds good on Sunday morning, it has no relevance on Tuesday evening when they are in the middle of a fight. They have no real idea what their new relationship with Christ is really about. Jesus' personal presence with Brian and Kara in the midst of conflict is never acknowledged. They don't stop to ask him for help because they don't think of him as a person. They think of him more in terms of a lawyer who has managed to keep them from going to jail. Now that they are past that danger, they don't keep relating to him.

What *are* the implications of these things for Brian and Kara—and for us? It means that each of us can have hope when we get out of bed in the morning; we know that the Lord of heaven and earth is truly our Father. This is what it means to live by faith. Imagination takes us to the mountaintop of God's grace so we can see our struggles and challenges from the vantage point of his relentless love for us.

Imagine Kara connecting with Christ personally each morning and talking to him like this: "Jesus, thank you for being with me right now and through this day. Because of you, I am never alone. Because of you, I don't have to manage the universe—or even Brian! Please give me your strength to entrust Brian to you; help me to love him in ways that will help both of us to see you and to love you and each other."

Imagine Brian uttering words like, "Father, I know I have looked to things such as status and success for a sense of well-being. I've grown depressed when I couldn't achieve them. I have minimized your immense love for me in Christ. For that, I deserve your condemnation. But because of what Christ has done for me, I am accepted by you—not only tolerated but also wonderfully embraced by you. As I take each step today, help me to know that you are for me and with me. While I may struggle with depression, I am first and foremost your beloved child. Let these truths and your personal presence give me courage to move into my life and my relationship with Kara."

In these little vignettes, Brian and Kara are putting faith into action. They are communing with the unseen God because their imagination is enabling them to see reality. As Kara's friend steered them to people in the church who could help them, this is what Kara and Brian began to learn how to do.

God's Presence and Provision

What else do Brian and Kara need to see with the eyes of faith imagination? When struggles remain and life does not change overnight, it is easy for confusion and helplessness to settle in. These things cloud the imagination. They lead us to think that the struggles of our lives are unique, that no one understands, and that we are all alone. Trying harder only seems to aggravate the problem. We try our best to figure it out, but we still don't come up with any answers.

When we are in this place of neediness and discouragement, we want answers and strategies, but God gives us something better. God's provision simply can't be reduced to answers and strategies because his provision is tied to his presence. God knows that our need is much bigger and deeper than what we think will satisfy it. So he not only gives us practical advice; he gives us himself. *He* is our wisdom. *He* is our strength. *He* is our forgiveness. *He* is our Father. As Moses said in Exodus 33:15: "If your Presence does not go with us, do not send us up from here." Moses knew that if God is not near, all the strategies and techniques in the world won't help against overwhelming odds. Jesus takes this reality of presence and provision a step further in John 14:15–20. He says that he will not just be near us or with us but *in* us.

"If you love me, you will obey what I command. And I will ask the Father, and he will give you another Counselor to be with you forever—the Spirit of truth. The world cannot accept him, because it neither sees him nor knows him. But you know him, for he lives with you and will be in you. I will not leave you as orphans; I will come to you. Before long, the world will not see me anymore, but you will see me. Because I live, you also will live. On that day you will realize that I am in my Father, and you are in me, and I am in you."

Jesus describes his presence in terms of a family relationship when he says he will not leave us as orphans. Brian and Kara need to face their struggles with the knowledge that God, the ultimate source of all they need, is living inside them. In the midst of their difficulty, Brian and Kara do not have to despair and feel alone in their struggles; God is present. They don't have to resort to speaking words that hurt; they can speak words that heal. They don't have to succumb to disappointment, bitterness, and vengeance; they can choose to be patient, kind, forgiving, and compassionate. They can encourage rather than condemn. They can bear each other's burdens and serve each other with joy. The promises of new potential don't have to be seen through jaded eyes; they can be received in a way that fosters new, heartfelt hope and obedience, even if things don't get better right away. Why? Because their imagination now sees not simply a restored marriage, but a deeper, moment-by-moment personal relationship with God. Ultimately, this is why Brian and Kara have been created and redeemed.

The stakes are high: the reality our imagination embraces is the reality we will live by. If we are not captured by the truth of living in a deeply personal relationship with God, we will shrink our expectations and dreams down to the size of our own selfish wants, desires, and strategies. This is what has happened to Brian and Kara, and it often happens to the rest of us. The pressure to attain success as others had defined it was crushing Brian. Now he was seeing that God was making him into something far more glorious: God was making him like Christ. Kara had allowed her vision for life to shrink to the size of controlling her little corner of the universe. But now she was seeing for the first time that God was already in control. She could trust him to change Brian because she was beginning to trust him to change her.

What Is God Doing in My Life?

When we don't see our identity in Christ or his presence and provision for us, we wind up envisioning a God too busy to care about us. Prayer becomes little more than a spiritual 911 call. To get God's attention, we "make the call" so that God will wake up, see our needs, act in our behalf, and provide rescue. But once he shows up and does what we think he should, we assume that he then retreats to take care of other pressing matters until our next call.

This flies in the face of the reality of who God is and how he works, but it is how Brian and Kara had tended to view God. To them, he was distant and inactive. In fact, Kara had wondered aloud why God had not done something to help her marriage. Brian wondered why God did not lift his depression. Their view of God's passivity was a principal ingredient in their abiding hopelessness. So was their focus on circumstances, which kept them from seeing their deeper heart issues of success, control, and acceptance that needed to be addressed by the power of the gospel.

Once again, the Scriptures enlarge our imagination by helping us see things we don't normally see. The Scriptures increase our awareness of a God who is near, willing, and able to save. In Psalm 121, the psalmist points to God's abiding presence and tireless activity on our behalf:

> I lift up my eyes to the hills—
>> where does my help come from?
> My help comes from the LORD,
>> the Maker of heaven and earth.
> He will not let your foot slip—
>> he who watches over you will not slumber;
> indeed, he who watches over Israel
>> will neither slumber nor sleep.
> The LORD watches over you—
>> the LORD is your shade at your right hand;
> the sun will not harm you by day,
>> nor the moon by night.
> The LORD will keep you from all harm—
>> he will watch over your life;
> the LORD will watch over your coming and going
>> both now and forevermore.

The same picture of God is seen in the life and words of the apostle Paul. In the midst of many struggles and pressures, Paul says in Romans 8:28–39:

> And we know that in all things God works for the good of those who love him, who have been called according to his purpose. For those God foreknew he also predestined to be conformed to the likeness of his Son, that he might be the firstborn among many brothers. And those he predestined, he also called; those he called, he also justified; those he justified, he also glorified. What, then, shall we say in response to this? If God is for us, who can be against us? He who did not spare his own Son, but gave him up for us all—how will he not also, along with him, graciously give us all things? Who will bring any charge against those whom God has chosen? It is God who justifies. Who is he that condemns? Christ Jesus, who died—more than that, who was raised to life—is at the right hand of God and is also interceding for us. Who shall separate us from the love of Christ? Shall trouble or hardship or persecution or famine or nakedness or danger or sword? As it is written:
> "For your sake we face death all day long;
>   we are considered as sheep to be slaughtered."
> No, in all these things we are more than conquerors through him who loved us. For I am convinced that neither death nor life, neither angels nor demons, neither the present nor the future, nor any powers, neither height nor depth, nor anything else in all creation, will be able to separate us from the love of God that is in Christ Jesus our Lord.

How radically these verses confront our feeble imaginations! When we are in trouble, our tendency is to think that God is nowhere to be found and that we must fix things ourselves. When our vision of reality is this small, our attempts to fix things often make the trouble more troubling. We either want to fix the wrong things or fix the right things in the wrong way.

The Bible not only tells us that God works continuously; it also tells us how he works and what he is working on. This gives us hope and gives our work purpose and direction. When we start working off the same script as God, we function in ways that are truly redemptive. If God forgives, we must work to forgive. If he is working to make someone a better person, we should do what we can to encourage those changes. If God is working to make peace, we are to be peacemakers. If God daily bears our burdens, we want to help shoulder the burdens of others. If God is working to produce hearts of worship in us, we should seek to stimulate adoration in one another. In short, we are called to help one another see the unseen reality of our active, present, and personal God. God's work is driven by an agenda so much grander than simply making our lives better. He wants to remake us into his likeness. And that likeness can be seen in Jesus.

Many explanations could be offered to Brian and Kara about why things have gone wrong and how they can try to fix them. But explanations alone will not bring them to a new place in their marriage. Explanation by itself may bring temporary insight and change but nothing that lasts. The vastness of God's glory needs to loom so large before their eyes that they can see their problems in proper perspective. The courage to hope for lasting change is only as big as the God that their imagination—and ours—is able to see. When we see our identity in Christ, God's presence and provision, and what he is doing in the process, we are willing and able to do things we wouldn't do otherwise. Brian and Kara are beginning to do this in small but important ways.

Explanation, while an important aspect of change, is not sufficient. It must be fueled by imagination. Eugene Peterson captures the vital interplay between the two:

> We have a pair of mental operations, imagination and explanation, designed to work in tandem. When the gospel is given robust and healthy expression, the two work in graceful synchronicity. Explanation pins things down so that we can handle and use them—obey and teach, help and guide. Imagination opens things up so that we can grow into maturity—worship and adore, exclaim and honor, follow and trust. Explanation restricts and defines and holds down; imagination expands and lets loose. Explanation keeps our feet on the ground; imagination lifts our heads into the clouds. Explanation puts us in harness; imagination

catapults us into mystery. Explanation reduces life to what can be used; imagination enlarges life into what can be adored.[1]

Living in God's Big Sky Country

As you have been reading, maybe you've been thinking, *Okay, Paul and Tim, this sounds good, but how do I stimulate my imagination?* How do you stimulate your imagination in any area of life? If you have a vision for decorating your house, you buy decorating magazines and pore over them until you get an idea of what you want to do. If you want to take a vacation, you sit down with someone who has been where you want to go. You talk about his trip, gaining insight and excitement about what you can do when you get there. You will probably get travel brochures or look at the pictures from your friend's trip.

It is not enough for Brian and Kara to work on their marriage; they need to work on their imaginations. God has given them ways to do that. He has provided simple means that stimulate and enlarge their imaginations to see what they need to see. These means are prayer, truth, other believers, worship, and the sacraments. We are tempted to minimize those means because they seem so ordinary. And when we approach them without a clear sense of why they were given, we can miss the profound impact they should have on us.

Bible study and personal reading fall flat when we miss what Bible study and reading are meant to do. They are intended to be a means, not an end. The purpose of Bible study is to give me a vision of the God who is my Savior and with whom I am in relationship. Bible study is intended to stimulate worship, but so often it is focused on theology and rules. My relationships with my brothers and sisters in the body of Christ are intended to stimulate our collective appreciation of God's greatness and grace, but so often relationships become an end in themselves, serving our desires for acceptance. The Lord's Supper is a rich experience where spiritual truths are laid before us in tangible ways. It is intended to stir our imaginations to see the grace of God through taste, touch, and sight. But many times the Lord's Supper becomes nothing more than a ritual we perform by rote.

---

1. Eugene Peterson, *Subversive Spirituality* (Grand Rapids: Eerdmans, 1997), 167.

Many other things God provides can stir up our faith imagination: hymns and songs, sermons, seminars, poetry, allegory, physical creation, and short-term mission trips, to name a few. The natural world should stimulate our imagination. The life and ministry of the body of Christ should expand our faith and worship. In the midst of life's struggles and opportunities, we all need to ask how our imaginations can be stimulated to see and worship God. We should also look for the means God has given us to make this happen.

The reality your imagination sees is the reality that will shape your words, actions, attitudes, and relationships. The question is not, "Has God made adequate provision?" The question is, "Do we see him? Are we responding to one another not only on the basis of personal strength, the size of the problem, or our track record, but on the basis of what God has provided?"

Brian and Kara look a lot like us. Like them, we forget that it is in the little moments of life that spiritual battles are lost and won. We tend to minimize the significance of the daily, moment-by moment skirmishes with outward circumstances and inward sin. But Brian and Kara are beginning to see what it is like to depend on Christ in those little moments. Brian may still struggle with depression, but Christ is present with him, helping Brian to see himself through new eyes. Kara is on a similar journey. She is relinquishing her need to be in control and trusting God to make all things new—even her! While much change is still needed, the eyes of their hearts are being opened to see how wide, deep, broad, and long the love and glory of Christ are. As they see through eyes of faith (or the eyes of reality), Christ is changing them from one degree of glory to another. This is truly amazing, yet it is exactly what God has said is reality all along.

How are you viewing reality? Are you growing in your ability to see the unseen? The apostle Paul encourages and commands us to do that in Ephesians 5:14:

> "Wake up, O sleeper,
>   rise from the dead,
> and Christ will shine on you."

Leader's Guide

This course has been designed to help people

- Value their relationships
- Understand why relationships are difficult
- Rejoice in God's grace that can bring healthy, godly relationships

This leader's guide has been designed to help you teach the truths of Scripture that can bring healthy, godly relationships. The lessons are designed to be interactive and to stimulate participation and thoughtful self-evaluation for each participant. The course can be used with any size group, and suggestions are offered to ensure full participation even from larger groups.

Reviewing this leader's guide is the first step in preparing yourself to teach this material. Be sure that you understand the material yourself and make it your own so that you can clearly and persuasively present it to others. Directions and suggestions for the leader are in the outside margins.

The Course Outline provides a brief overview of the key points and activities so you can prepare for each lesson, and each lesson has its own elements that help guide the instruction and learning. Time parameters are included, and each lesson is designed to be seventy-five to ninety minutes long. This can be adjusted depending on the needs and time provided. One option is to assign a portion of the lessons to be done at home. If you think you may have leftover time, you could be prepared to discuss or have them begin one of the activities under Make It Real. The suggested times are guidelines, and you will need to make decisions about allowing more or less time. View the material as a tool that God will use, and let *him* use it how *he* desires. This requires you to be prayerful and in close connection with the Lord.

Some lessons require advanced planning from you. The lesson will state this at the beginning in the top margin, but it would be optimal for you to review these lessons well in advance so you can be fully prepared (see lessons 1, 4, 9, 10, 12). Also, be aware some lessons ask participants to do an activity on their own to prepare for future lessons (end of lessons 2, 7, 10).

Central Points, Applications, and Big Questions

Allowing for discussion always brings the possibility of getting off topic. Each lesson provides a central point and personal and relational applications at the beginning and end that can help guide the focus and bring a group back that veers from the main principles. Also, a Big Question is asked at the beginning to guide a lesson's applications. You may want to ask the question at the end of each lesson as well. You could even write the question on poster board or another easy display to be visible during the entire lesson. If you need to adjust the lessons, use the Big Question as a means of deciding how to best make adjustments. Your goal is for every participant to be able to understand the question and answer it.

Review

Reviewing previous lessons and the work the participants did on their own will reinforce key concepts and will encourage participants to do the work necessary at home (Make It Real questions). Review questions should also stimulate discussion and allow you, the leader, to receive feedback from the participants. You want as much participation as possible so consider whether creating smaller groups is best for discussing the review questions.

Opening Activity

Every lesson has an Opening Activity designed to get participants to begin thinking about the topic for the lesson.

Main Content

Between the Opening Activity and Closing Activity is the main content. Typically thirty to forty minutes long, this is the heart of the lesson and includes readings, questions, activities, and discussion. Some questions are asked only for participants to respond to for themselves; these are written directly into the readings. Most questions are meant to be answered with the group and responded to aloud; a large question mark indicates these. Possible answers to questions are written in brackets and are in the margins. Your goal is for participants to participate. Allow time for people to think. If no one is answering, try asking the question in a different way. It is good to seek even multiple answers. If one person seems to always answer, try calling on different people. Don't force anyone to answer.

Closing Activity

The closing activity is designed as a way to review and to put the main ideas of the lesson into immediate practice.

Make It Real

This section is designed to extend the main ideas and for participants to apply them in their own lives. It typically involves more reflective exercises. It may help your group if you share what you gained or did for one of the items in the Make It Real section as part of the next lesson's review. If you want the group to be sincere and open, you will need to model that for them and set the atmosphere by what you share.

COURSE OUTLINE

Lesson 1: Relationships and the Nature of God (90 mins.)
Requires advanced planning; see Opening Activity

Central Point: Because God himself is a community, he created and intends for us to live in community so that we may be a reflection of him.

Opening Activity: (15–25 mins.) Brainstorm any words that come to mind when you hear the word *relationships.*
It would be good to write them down—even better if it were a large sheet of paper or board to refer to during the lesson and at the closing activity.

Q1 (10–15 mins.): You may want to have each participant answer the first part of the question (which side) and then take volunteers to answer the second part (why).

Relational Profiles (15–20 mins.)

Q1a Answer: The one who seeks isolation may want to just sit and read, relax; while the one who seeks immersion may want lots of activities to do together.

Q1b Answer: The isolationist can feel smothered while the immersionist feels rejected. Because both feel like their expectations are unmet, they both feel frustrated and disappointed, which may eventually lead to anger between them.

Q2a Answer: They might spend every waking moment together and ignore other relationships.

Q2b Answer: Because they are so dependent on each other, they can be easily hurt when the other does not meet their expectation, which can lead them to be highly critical of the other. They can feel discouraged because, no matter how hard they try, they can never measure up to the other person's expectations. This kind of relationship is exhausting because much energy is spent dealing with minor offenses.

Q3a Answer: They might both spend time alone, each reading a different book.

Q3b Answer: Because they desire safety but also connection—because we are all designed to desire connection—they feel empty and disappointed.

This could be a good time to pray and ask God to help each person in the group to be honest and to seek what he desires for their relationships.

Our Communal God (30 mins.) Ask the questions to the group and solicit answers. Possible answers and guidelines are:

Q1 Answer: Jesus is praying for all those who will believe in him, and he prays for their unity—that they would be one. It is relevant that as Jesus looks back on his public ministry and all it was meant to accomplish, and looks forward to the cross and all it was ordained to produce, his focus is riveted on community! Of all the things Christ could pray for at this moment, he prays for the unity of his people.

Q2 Answer: Jesus wants us to have the same community with God and with others that he has with the Father and Spirit. We can see this community also in Genesis 1:26, where God speaks in the plural, "Let us make man . . . ." God knows how to help us with our struggles with community because he is a community. We tend to think of God as an individual; but, while God is one, the Bible also says he exists in three persons: the trinity. God himself is a model of loving, cooperative, unified community where diversity is an asset and not a liability.

Q3 Answer: It means we were created to be in community; we were created as social beings. In Genesis 2:18 as God looks at his creation before the fall, he says, "It is not good for man to be alone." Community with one another is not only a duty; it is an aspect of our humanity.

Q4 Answer: Human community is to be a means of reflecting God's glory to the world, that the world may believe in God the Father and God the Son. Furthermore, God has a purpose for our relationships; therefore, our relationships must be shaped by what God intends and not by what we want.

Q5 Answer: Because we are flawed; we are sinners; we can't manufacture true community on our own. Sin's self-centeredness cuts us off from God and others.

Q6 Answer: Jesus prays that we would have community with God. We are invited to be a part of this divine community! And it is out of this community that we can experience community with one another. In fact, we can't move toward community with one another until we have been drawn into community with God.

Q7 Answer: (1) v. 22, "I have given them the glory that you gave me, that they may be one as we are one." It's possible Jesus is referring to the Holy Spirit as the glory he has given to us. If so, it means God has given us a way, in spite of the ongoing presence of sin, to be empowered to have meaningful relationships. The Spirit who allowed Christ to minister in a fallen world is the same Spirit who dwells within us to allow us to minister in a fallen world. (2) Christ is facing death on a cross so that our relationship to God can be restored and so that our relationships with others can be glorifying to him.

Q8 Answer: Some answers may include: we are dependent upon someone from the moment we are born; we seek out human relationships; as teens we seek acceptance of our peers; as young adults we begin to desire deeper, more committed relationships; we have a web of communities we function in—church, neighborhood, schools, family, work—our fondest memories and deepest hurts often involve relationships; we grieve at the loss of a loved one, even when we know he or she is with the Lord.

Closing Activity: (15 mins.) Identify and add any words that should be the focus of our thoughts about relationships.

Show the words that were generated during the opening activity time, and ask, "Do we have any words here that should be the focus of our thoughts about relationships? Are there any words you feel we should add?" Don't discredit any opinions about words that should be the focus, but you might want to facilitate them toward words such as *work, important, God-pleasing, human, God's image, necessary*. After marking words that should be the focus of defining relationships, allow time for participants to write their answers to question 1. You may want to ask if anyone wants to share his or her answers to the question.

Lesson 2: Relationships—The Problem and the Solution (90 mins.)

Review (10 mins.)

Central Point: Our problems in relationships have everything to do with sin inside us, and our potential to overcome the problems has everything to do with Christ.

Opening Activity: Questions (5 mins.)

Inside Out, Upside Down

Exploring the Problem (10–15 mins.): Encourage the participants to be creative. There are no right or wrong answers. Allow participants to share their answers.

Read Romans 7:21–25 (10 mins.)

Q1 Answer: Some key ideas include the *law of sin*—sin is an inescapable principle in our lives that we will never be free from until we are made perfect; *war*—sin is a continual inner conflict, battling against God's law; *prisoner*—though we may want to do what is right, often sin pulls us and removes our freedom; *rescue*—our sin requires an outside helper; *body of death*—sin brings death and separation both physically and relationally.

Conclusion: Be sure the participants grasp this conclusion. You may want to repeat it, have a couple different participants read it aloud, or have the whole group read it aloud together.

The Basic Effects of Sin (30 mins.)

Q1a. Answer: When things got tough, they immediately defaulted to a what-is-best-for-me? position rather than a what-is-God-doing-in-and-through-us? perspective.

Q2a. Answer: They respond to each other by trying to take control—Shane tries to dominate Kristin with criticism and demands; Kristin tries to control Shane with isolation and silence.

Q3a. Answer: They try to solve the problem on their own; they don't work together in dependency but move toward isolation and independence. They forget that God has not left them alone but has provided each the other to depend upon.

Q4a. Answer: It is very possible each thinks he or she is more righteous than the other. Each is quite aware of the other's sin and works hard to get the other to see it, too, rather than looking at his or her own heart and seeking the help that only the Savior can provide.

Q5a. Answer: With her girlfriends Kristin has replaced the community God wants her to have with Shane, and Shane has placed his energies and hope in his job. Neither is making the investments in the relationship they once loved to make.

Q6a. Answer: They don't listen to the other's view and perspective; they don't try to understand.

Allow time for the participants to examine the chart and examine their relationships.

What About the Bad Things People Do to Me? (5 mins.)

Q1 Answer: His Word, which provides wise principles and promises; his Spirit, who convicts us when we are wrong, empowers us to seek forgiveness, and enables us to show compassion and self-control; his body of believers who can correct and encourage us; baptism, which identifies us a child of God and a member of his body; the Lord's Supper, which reminds us to maintain our unity with God and with other members of his family.

Closing Activity: Exploring the Solution (10–15 mins.): Encourage the participants to be creative. There are no right or wrong answers. Allow participants to share their answers.

Preparation for lessons 3 and 4 home assignment

Lesson 3: Relationships—God's Workshop (80 mins.)

Review (15 mins.) You want every person to be able to be a part of the review. Consider the size of your group, and determine if dividing into smaller groups would be most effective for the review.

Central Point: God uses relationships to lead us into growth and sanctification.

Opening Activity: (5 mins.) Can you identify the underlying agenda in these statements? The agenda in each of these statements is what the person gets out of the relationship. It is ultimately self-centered.

Two Scriptural Themes (5 mins.)
  Q2a: Allow time for participants to think to themselves in answering this question.

Ephesians 4: God's Desire for Our Relationships (30–40 mins.) You could have the participants share their list that was made as the assignment for the end of lesson 2 or just give an overview— see Appendix A.
  A Call to Unity
  "There is one Spirit, one Lord, and one Father" Q1 Answer: Some examples are: Jesus was humble in becoming man and dying on the cross; the Father gently and patiently works out our salvation; the Holy Spirit forbears and abides with us even in the face of our sin, convicting and correcting but never condemning.
  Our Struggle and God's Agenda: Allow time for participants to answer the seven tendencies question to themselves.

Closing Activity: (15 mins.) Read the case study (Josh and Sara).

Q1 Answer: Some ideas could include: The problems began when they considered the move apart from including God's agenda, which would have meant researching churches before moving. They needed to place a priority on church relationships as God does. Another root of the problem is they are seeking churches based on their own agendas instead of seeking God to lead them to a church where they can be used in relationships. They are looking for comfort instead of looking to be used by God. They need to search their own hearts and be willing to humble themselves; they need to seek God to reveal how they can grow from this situation.

Q2 Answer: God wants to use the struggles of our relationships as a means for our growth and sanctification. Like a rock-climbing wall—it takes work, but the work is satisfying when you see where you began and where you ended up; obstacles are in the way but the obstacles are tools for getting to the top if you use them that way. Likewise, relationships are work but can be quite satisfying as we grow and mature, and our struggles are not obstacles but instruments in God's hands. If you look at your own character, you may find some of your deepest growth has been born out of great stress and trial.

Use with Appendix A

Lesson 4: Two Foundation Stones (80–90 mins.)

Requires advanced planning; see Closing Activity

Review (10 mins.) Again, you want as much participation as possible, so consider whether creating smaller groups is best for discussing the review questions.

Central Point: Good relationships are built on remembering who we are in God's eyes and worshipping God for who he is.

Opening Activity: Case Study (Matt and Rob)—Why do we struggle with one person one way and a different person another way?

The Two Foundation Stones

Remembering Who You Are **(20 mins.)**: Provide time for participants to reread the scenario and to identify an answer and then to share ideas with the group.

Q1 Answer: Rob seems to be getting his identity from success and achievement but feels as if Matt is in his way; Rob seems to be resting his identity on gaining respect and acceptance from Matt, but feels as if Matt doesn't need or appreciate him.

Biblical identities forgotten and remembered: Participants do not need to use the same wording that is provided. Try to understand the concept they are explaining and accept answers that are not necessarily the same as the ones given here as guidelines.

Sarah and Abraham: Their true identity was as chosen children of God and inheritors of God's promises. They made themselves the fulfiller of the promise. The reaction was to take control and resulted in conflict and hostility.

Peter: His true identity was saved by grace through faith; he was God's messenger for all the nations. He instead made himself a slave to the law again and dependent on the judgments of others. As a result there was conflict and the Gentile brothers were rejected.

Moses: He remembered he was God's instrument and was able to lead the people out of Egypt into the promised land.

David: He remembered he was God's servant and that God was on his side, and he was able to face Goliath and defeat him.

Paul and Silas: They remembered they were in God's hands—loved and seen by him at all times—and so they were able to sing hymns as they sat in prison.

Q2: Allow time for participants to write down an answer.

Remembering Who God Is **(20 mins.)**

Q1a Answer: That they are not a mistake in any way. The shape of their body, the sound of their voice, their personality, and their intellectual and natural abilities are all designed by God—they were crafted by a gloriously wise Creator.

Q1b Answer: My role is only to love and appreciate the creation (persons) and point them in the direction of the one who can change them (their Creator.)

Q2 Answer: We need to respect and appreciate those differences.

Q3 Answer: We are all sinners, and we are all saved through faith in Christ Jesus.

Closing Activity: (30 mins.) Worship. You could do a couple of ideas here. You could invite someone within the group to prepare a worship time of singing and praising God, or you could ask someone from outside the group. The worship time could be a time of praying when the group gives thanks to God for who they are: "God, I thank you that I am _____" and praising God for who he is. You could invite people to stand and complete the statement, "God, you are _____." Songs could focus on attributes of God or on songs of thanks for what God has done for us.

Lesson 5: Relationships and Communication (75 mins.)

Review (15 mins.)

Central Point: As Christ's ambassadors, we represent him every time we speak.

Opening Activity: (15–20 mins.) Ambassador—Game simulation. See Appendix B for game instructions.

A Radical Commitment to the Call of Christ (20–25 mins.)

Q1 Answer: ambassadors

Q2 Answer: We are God's representatives here on earth. It focuses on God's rule as King.

Q2a Answer: As God's representatives, we speak on his behalf.

Q3 Answer: reconciliation—see also 2 Corinthians 5:15

God's Perspective on Our Words

Our Words Have Power

Q1 Answer: Words can kill a spirit, a dream, kill an attitude or perspective. Killing words are angry, hurtful, slanderous, selfish, bitter, divisive, and demeaning forms of talk.

Q2 Answer: They can give life to a spirit or a dream; they can give birth to an attitude or perspective. Life-giving words encourage, comfort, make peace, build up, unify, and show love and gratitude.

The World of Talk Is a World of Trouble

Read James 3:2b—"If anyone is never at fault in what he says, he is a perfect man, able to keep his whole body in check."

Q1 Answer: We will never be perfect in our speech; our words are an indicator of our spiritual maturity; our words reveal our need for God's grace.

Word Problems Are Heart Problems

Q1 Answer: our hearts

Q2 Answer: The condition of our heart is the problem. Our problem with words is not primarily a matter of vocabulary, skill, or timing; it is always the attitude, thoughts, desires, emotions, and purposes that dwell within us.

Before the closing activity, pray together, asking forgiveness for our use of words and asking God for grace to use words for his purposes.

Closing Activity: Giving Encouragement (15 mins.)

Use with Appendix B

Lesson 6: Conflict (75–85 mins.)

Review/Opening Activity: (10 mins. + 1–2 mins./group) Case Study (Ashley and Hannah)—Evaluate Hannah and Ashley's conflict. What is the root of the problem? What will restore the relationship?

If possible divide your group into smaller groups of three to five to read and discuss the opening activity; and then allow each group to share its answers with the whole group.

Q1 Answer: Though Hannah's words were subtle, they were the overflow of her heart, which means they were calculated to make Ashley look bad. The desire to look better than Ashley was already in Hannah's heart before the words were spoken. Hannah did not see Ashley's temperament as God's sovereign design but as sin. She did not extend grace to Ashley as God would want her to do, and she did not speak out of Ashley's best interest. Ashley did not look to be Christ's ambassador to Hannah and speak in the best manner. Instead of looking for God's redemptive power, Ashley took on the role of judge and accuser. Ashley did not move toward the relationship as Christ's ambassador but distanced herself and her feelings from Hannah.

Central Point: Relationships inevitably bring conflict but also growth.

Facing Conflicts Head On (30 mins.) Ask, "What is your tendency: to avoid conflict or to rush into it? Do you move into conflict with a God-centered perspective?"

The Cause and Cure of Ungodly Conflict

Q1 Answer: our own desires; not getting what we want

Q2: You may want to give some time for participants to reread and consider which of these desires really does tend to overshadow their desire for godliness.

Q3: Everyone should answer this question because it is important that we all are aware of the desires that tend to drive conflict in our lives. It is not appropriate to only blame the other person or to only blame the situation. Being aware of our heart's sinful desires can help diffuse or avoid conflict. Participants do not need to provide a lengthy explanation but should at least answer which one(s).

Q4 Answer: It is to make yourself and your selfish desires more important than God's glory.

Q5 Answer: We can only be adulterous because we are married to God. He loves us as in a marriage relationship. We are also considered God's friends. Though God is absolutely holy, he still loves us as his bride and accepts us as his friends.

What Does God Do to People Who Forsake Him for Something Else?

Q1 Answer: other people!

Let's Get Practical (15 mins.)

Q1 Answer: warn, encourage, and help

Q2 Answer: be patient, kind, thankful, joyful, and not vengeful

Closing Activity: (20 mins.) Case Study (Troy and Angela)—What do Troy and Angela need to think about and then do to resolve the conflict and restore the relationship?

This can be done in a few different ways. You could have participants write out their answers individually first and then meet in small groups to compare; you could have them meet in small groups to develop an answer and then share with the whole group; you could ask them to turn to someone next to them and share verbally and then ask for answers from the whole group. There is an answer in Appendix C.

Lesson 7: Forgiveness—Absorbing the Cost (80 mins.)

Review (20 mins.)

Central Point: As a community of forgiven people, we are called to practice forgiveness.

Opening Activity: (15 mins.) Before defining forgiveness, pray, asking God to search your hearts and help you understand and practice true biblical forgiveness. If your group is able, you could have them recite the Lord's Prayer together as well.

What is forgiveness? What can cause forgiving to be so difficult? You could have people share their definition with someone next to them and then ask for definitions to be shared with the whole group. Some answers might include: feeling hurt; like forgiving them would justify or approve of their sin; forgiveness feels as if you are taking away justice, letting them "off the hook"; they don't deserve it, and so forth.

What Does It Mean to Forgive? (30 mins.) Ask participants to share a word or phrase that sticks out to them after reading the parable. Limit the amount of time and explanations, however, so that you can continue to move forward.

Forgiveness Is Costly, but Not Forgiving Is More Costly

Q1 Answer: God is going to treat us the same way we treat others.

Q2 Answer: Forgiveness has no limits. We are always to forgive even when it is the same, endlessly repeated offense. Forgiveness is also something we need to continue to practice even when we are dealing with an offense we have already forgiven.

Forgiveness is not forgetting. Ask the group to try and not think about an elephant—they probably immediately pictured an elephant when you said it.

Q3: This is a rather personal question, but it can be good for people to express thoughts aloud. It will also encourage participants as they hear others struggle with similar feelings. Don't allow answers to these questions to lead to gossip; ask that the specifics be left out.

Forgiveness has a vertical and a horizontal dimension.

Q4 Answer: Read Mark 11:25: "And when you stand praying, if you hold anything against anyone, forgive him, so that your Father in heaven may forgive you." This verse is in the context of worship.

It relates to our vertical relationship to God. This is the attitude we must always have before God—an attitude of forgiveness toward others. This is nonnegotiable. We do not have the right to withhold forgiveness and harbor bitterness in our hearts. Read Luke 17:3: "If your brother sins, rebuke him, and if he repents, forgive him." This verse considers our horizontal relationship and the act of reconciliation. While we are to have attitudes of forgiveness before the Lord, we can only grant forgiveness to other people if they repent and admit they have sinned against us. Even if they never do this, we are called to maintain an attitude of forgiveness toward the offenders. This means Grace can say to John, "Before the Lord, I have forgiven you and I will not make you pay for what you have done." But she can only grant forgiveness to John and pursue reconciliation if he admits he has sinned and asks for forgiveness. Grace may long for reconciliation between her and John, but ultimately she cannot make reconciliation occur.

Asking For and Granting Forgiveness (15 mins.)

Dialogue between Andy and Melissa: Andy actually blames the fight on Melissa! He implied that the problem was not that he yelled at her, but that she was too sensitive about it. Melissa responds by accepting the blame for Andy's sin and then excusing her own response. The great problem here is that no one admits any sin and no one offers forgiveness.

Allow time for the group to rewrite the dialogue and then ask some to share how they rewrote it. Ask the group for any other changes or additions. It should sound something like the following:

> "Melissa, I am sorry for yelling at you. What I did was wrong. Will you forgive me?"
>
> "Thank you, Andy; yes, I forgive you. Will you forgive me for being sarcastic toward you?"
>
> "Yes, Melissa, I forgive you."

Melissa should not say that it is okay because it is not okay for someone to sin against another person.

Q1 Answer: Yes. An apology is appropriate when you have done something by accident. For example, if I accidentally spill a cup of coffee on you, I should say, "I am very sorry I did that," and help you get cleaned up. But if I purposefully threw coffee on you because I was irritated, that is not an accident. That is sin and requires me to name the sin, confess that I was wrong, and ask for forgiveness.

Closing Activity: NA

Preparation for lesson 8 home assignment

Lesson 8: Hope in the Middle (80–90 mins.)

Review (10 mins.)

Central Point: Our relationships will never be perfect; because of Christ, not only can we make it through the difficulties, but he can use us as instruments of his grace.

Opening Activity: (15 mins.) What do you like most: being at the beginning, in the middle, or at the end of something? Why?

Because it is safe, this is a good question to ask each participant or to specifically ask any participants who tend to be quieter.

Answer: We often like the beginning because there is a sense of hope and potential; we can be dreamers. Or we like the end because we feel relief, gratitude, and a sense of accomplishment; the sacrifices and difficulties seem worth it. Usually the middle of something is the most difficult because that is where the true work lies. Dreams and expectations morph into a desire to just survive. We hear most of the complaints and make most of our compromises in the middle of something.

Relationships in the Middle (20 mins.)

Q1a Answer: Answers may include that it is comforting to know God is in full control and has a plan that is for our good and for his glory, that God will not give us more than we can bear (1 Cor. 10), that God is our Shepherd and will guide us.

Q2a Answer: Answers may include that though people are flawed, Jesus is not and we can have a relationship with him; Jesus is faithful and will not give up on us or the other person; we can expect to live in harmony in the fulfilled kingdom of God.

Q3a Answer: Answers may include that even difficulty is sent and used by God for our own good in order to refine and mature us (James 1), God is an ever-present help in times of trouble, we can pray, and Jesus is an advocate on our behalf.

Q4a Answer: Answers may include that God gives us grace to do his will; the fruit of the Spirit can increase as we remain in Christ (John 15).

The Hardship of Relationships in the Middle

Q1: Any response is legitimate here. Some may feel overwhelmed or as if they can't do it. Actually this is how God planned it. Relationships will take us beyond the boundaries of our strength, beyond our natural abilities, beyond our acquired wisdom and will to succeed. Relationships will push us beyond the limits of our ability to love, serve, and forgive. Relationships will challenge our faith, exhaust us, and in certain situations leave us disappointed and discouraged. This is exactly as God intends it. When we begin to give up on ourselves, we begin to rely on him. When we abandon our own little dreams, we begin to get excited about his plan. When our ways have blown up in our faces, we are willing to see the wisdom of his ways. Our relationships are not simply designed to make us interdependent with one another but to drive us to him in humble personal dependency. When we discover and confess how weak we are, we reach out for his grace.

Encouraging Others in the Middle (15 mins.)

Q1a Answer: Some ideas may include: "Hang on, you can make it," "It's not really as bad as you think," "You're not the only one who has to face this," "It's going to be okay," "This too will pass."

Q1b Answer: Such statements are not always true; they often provide only temporary comfort but never lead to lasting change—they can produce a temporary change of mood that melts away once the person faces the difficulty again.

Real Encouragement

1. Christ's Presence Answers: (a) the earth giving way and the mountains falling around us; (b) no fear—peace, stability, security; (c) because God is an ever-present help, our refuge and strength.

3. Our Potential in Christ Answer: (a) Our potential is Christ living in us, and he is wanting to help; our potential is not our wisdom, strength, or ability but our faith.

Closing Activity: (20 mins.) Small Group Sharing

Use with Appendix D

Lesson 9: Transforming Average Relationships into Great Relationships (60–90 mins.)

Requires advanced planning; see Closing Activity

Review (10 mins.)

Central Point: Whoever wants to be great must become a servant.

Opening Activity: (10 mins.) How many "one another" commands can you name? You could have the group call out as many as they can think of as you check off the ones they say using Appendix D, or you can create a list by writing down their answers.

Read Mark 10:35–45. (15 mins.)

Q1 Answer: Ultimately, they are all being self-focused.

Q2 Answer: The pathway to greatness is found in humility and focusing on and serving others.

The Actions of a Great Relationship

Q1 Answer: It means we are required to serve others; when we choose not to serve others but ourselves instead, we place ourselves above Christ—a servant is not above his master.

Q2 Answer: Jesus knows the hour had come for him to die on the cross for self-centered sinners. He knows the wrath of a just and holy God will soon fall on him. He knows a friend will betray him.

Q3 Answer: He serves his disciples. He does for his disciples what they should have done for him.

Q4 Answer: Answers may include that the world tells us we are great when we climb the ladder of power and influence, that happiness and fulfillment come from being served; Jesus' example is quite the opposite—that purpose and fulfillment come from serving others; that we are great when we humble ourselves.

Doing the Miraculous (5 mins.) After this section, take time to pray. Ask God for forgiveness and grace to serve as Jesus served.

Closing Activity: Serving Opportunities (10–30 mins. depending on the service and needs). Have prepared several needs that participants could meet through service, either immediately or sometime during the week. Examples are: a family who would benefit from childcare or a meal, someone who needs work done on a car or in their house, work that needs to be done at the church. For any that are done immediately, you could come back together and discuss how they all feel after having served. Use whatever time is available to put the opportunity into action (i.e., call the family and set up a time to help).

Use with Appendix E

Lesson 10: Time and Money (60–90 mins.)

Requires advanced planning; see Closing Activity

Review (10 mins.)

Central Point: God lavishes his resources and grace on us so that we may share them in the lives of others.

Opening Activity: (5 mins.) John Piper writes, "God is calling us to be conduits of his grace, not cul-de-sacs." What does John Piper mean? Q1 Answer: A conduit joins a source to another place. It allows for and facilitates a flow of something. A cul-de-sac is an ending place. God's grace and blessings are not meant to end with us but are intended to flow through us into the lives of others.

Money and People (15 mins.)
Q1 Answer: (1) so that we do not need to steal, (2) so we can share with those in need.

Time and People (10 mins.)
Q1: You can allow for some interaction here, but because of time try to avoid an immense discussion. You want to move the lesson to the following points.

Closing Activity: (30 mins.) Have paper, pens, and pencils available. Write a note of encouragement to someone.

Make It Real Q2: This could make a nice small-group activity. Choose a date to come together with all the clothes everyone is willing to get rid of and then take them to a local mission or Salvation Army or send them to a Third World country.

Preparation for lesson 11 home assignment

Lesson 11: Review Lessons 1–10: Application Case Study (Brian and Kara) (75–90 mins.)

Review (15 mins.)

Activity 1: (30 mins.) Using the principles in lesson 8, consider what you would say to Brian and Kara to encourage them.

Q1 Answer: (1) There is no quick fix—this is a deep problem, situated in a long history. (2) They may feel trying is useless and need to be given hope first. (3) They need to shift their focus so they are not consumed by hopelessness. (4) Providing encouragement and empathy will build trust and foster a nonjudgmental relationship between you and Kara/Brian; encouraging and empathizing will make them feel loved and understood and will help bring them to a point where they are ready to listen and accept help. (5) If you come across like you have all the answers and no problems, it will only fuel their feeling of aloneness and hopelessness.]

Q2: Allow time for the participants to think about their answers. You could even encourage them to write down some thoughts before they respond aloud. If you have a large group, and if it is possible, consider breaking into smaller groups of men and groups of women to share ideas and then come back as a whole group to share.

Q3: Have participants share their ideas on how to best encourage Brian and Kara. Make note of which ideas remind Brian and Kara of God's presence, God's promises, and God's potential. Make positive comments about what participants share. If participants seem stuck or if they miss one of the elements of encouragement, prompt them by asking one of the questions on the next page.

Q4 Answer: God's grace is evident in: their love for their children and for each other, their children alone, continued financial provisions, and even their struggles—all draw them to need him and to seek the true source of help.

Activity 2: (30 mins.) Take on the role of Brian or Kara. What change in your perspective will help you move toward God's grace? How will you need to view the conflict and difficulties? How will Kara need to view Brian and vice versa? How will their worship of God help change their perspective for change to begin? How will they need to view their identity for change to occur? What is the desire in their hearts that has led to conflict? How might forgiveness play a crucial role, and what should that forgiveness look like? What ways of serving will help bring about change and provide mutual support?

This may be a good time to break into smaller groups of two to five, depending on the size of the whole group. Consider assigning each group a different question to answer, have them return to the big group, and then share their answer with the large group. Another way could be to stay as a whole group and ask them which of those questions will need to be answered and understood first by Brian and Kara. There is no right or wrong question to begin with, but it will probably get the participants thinking about the answer to the question that either they know best or the answer to the question that God has been working on in them. Another possibility is to have the questions on cards and randomly give them to individuals. Provide time for them all to think of what an answer could be for the question they were given—they could even use their notes—and then to share their answers with the whole group.

Use with Appendix F

Lesson 12: Moving Out (60–90 mins.)

Requires advanced planning; see Closing Activity

Review: (15 mins.) This review is intended to allow participants an opportunity to express what God has done or is doing in their relationships. Don't be afraid to allow it to go beyond the fifteen minutes suggested.

Central Point: Our relationships are intended to attract others to the King.

Opening Activity: (10–15 mins.) Prayer

The Kingdom of God (5 mins.) At the end of this section, ask, "How does this make you feel?" to be able to have interaction and mutual encouragement. Answers may range from feeling privileged as a part of God's kingdom and his work to feeling overwhelmed by the responsibility and unworthy of the expectation.

The Visible Kingdom: Salt and Light (25 mins.)

Salt

Q1 Answer: We need to be in close contact with the world. Salt is only effective as a retardant to decay when it is in close contact with a substance. This is an uncomfortable call for us because it pulls us away from the comfort of relationships already transformed by the King. Yet we are most true to our identity and calling when we live in the midst of broken people. The call of the kingdom is a call into the world, never away from it. We are to be in the world, though not of it. Often, Christians have evaded the challenge of this call by defining their role as salt in negative terms. They have simply denounced bad things in the culture and been against rather than for the positive.

Q2 Answer: We are to be people of good character. Salt is only effective if it is salty! We are called to be people of great character so that when we come in contact with the world our character influences those around us. These qualities are not just about courage and conviction but humility and compassion as well. What we say is important, but how we say it is too. What we stand for is important, but who we are as we stand for those things is important too. If, by God's grace, we are truly "salty," God intends us to apply that salt to decayed relationships where it is most needed.

Light

Q1 Answer: We reveal truth, God, and his kingdom to the world.

Q2 Answer: Light has an attention-getting quality; it involves welcoming people in so that they can see that the kingdom has come. We welcome people in so that they can see the impact of the kingdom on our relationships. Our relationships are meant to be beacons in a dark world.

Q3 Answer: humility, patience, forgiveness, service, compassion

Participants will probably come up with the answers above, especially if you prompt them; but they may not add the following, which you should do. Another thing people may need to see is your own need for grace. People may not benefit as much from an I've-arrived-but-you-need-grace approach. It's in the context of your own sins, struggles, and weaknesses that the love and power of the King are most clearly seen. Both of us authors have had people live in our homes for a period of time. Invariably, our guests have said that the most helpful thing about the experience (in addition to the good things they observed) was the fact that they saw our sins and our daily need for grace. One mark of the kingdom is a humble awareness of the ongoing pull of sin and the daily cries for help that result.

Closing Activity: (30 mins.) Celebrating What God Has Done

This is a good opportunity to celebrate what God has done and to further relationships. Consider having a meal together or only desserts and a time to socialize. Include a prayer time or song time.

Appendices

B: Ambassadors Game Simulation. It may create a nice tie-in with the lesson if you give one person from Group C a statement to say to one of the people in Group A. For example, "Tell Steve he can ask you for twenty dollars at anytime and you will give it to him."